UNTIL THE
MESSIAH COMES

Other Books
in the Do-It-Yourself
Jewish Adventure Series
by Kenneth D. Roseman

THE CARDINAL'S SNUFFBOX

THE MELTING POT: *An Adventure in New York*

ESCAPE FROM THE HOLOCAUST

THE TENTH OF AV

THE OTHER SIDE OF THE HUDSON:
A Jewish Immigrant Adventure

UNTIL THE MESSIAH COMES

A Russian-Jewish Adventure

Kenneth D. Roseman, Ph.D.

UAHC Press
New York

*To all those Jews of the Former Soviet Union who,
in spite of seven decades of great oppression and
hostility, preserved their Jewish identity so that
it can now flower in freedom.*

Acknowledgements

Thank you to the many people at the UAHC Press who helped
bring this book into being: Debra Hirsch Corman; Liane Broido;
Kathy Parnass; Stuart Benick; Ken Gesser; Hara Person; and
Michelle Young.

Maps by Steven J. Davies, Mapping Specialists Limited.

Library of Congress Cataloging-in-Publication Data
Roseman, Kenneth.
    Until the Messiah comes/ by Kenneth D. Roseman.
      p. cm.—(The Do-it-yourself Jewish adventure series)
    Includes bibliographical references.
    Summary: The reader's decisions control the course of the action
as various Jewish characters in eastern Europe at the turn of the
twentieth century decide where their lives will take them.
    ISBN 0-8074-0706-2 (pbk. : alk. paper)
    1. Jews—Europe, Eastern Juvenile fiction. 2. Plot-your-own
stories. [1. Jews—Europe, Eastern Fiction. 2. Plot-your-own
stories.]   I. Title. II. Series: Roseman, Kenneth. Do-it-yourself
Jewish adventure series.
PZ7.R71863Un   1999
[Fic]—DC21   99-26328
                                         CIP

Dear Reader:

You are about to embark on a great adventure. Using your imagination and creativity, you can actually go back in time about a hundred years and transport yourself through space from your home or school to the eastern parts of Europe.

This adventure is about history. But that does not mean dry facts or irrelevant stories. The history in this book is about people who may be your grandparents or great-grandparents. You see, most American-Jewish families have ancestors who lived through this time and these events, and many millions of other families were also affected by them. (You might even ask some of the older members of your family if they remember these times and if they have some stories to add to the ones here in this book.)

Obviously, no one historical person could possibly have had all the experiences described in this book. I have taken some liberties (authors do that kind of thing) to make the action more exciting. But you should know that everything in this book did really happen in Russia and its neighboring countries between 1881 and 1918. This is a book about true events.

When you encounter words in bold that you do not understand, people you do not know about, or places that seem foreign to you, look them up either in the glossary or on the maps. You can also find many of them in encyclopedias and other reference works in your library.

This is also a book about real people, people who were not so different from you. They faced interesting and sometimes difficult decisions in their lives, and the history in this book is the history of the choices they made. As you read this book, you will make choices too, so you can understand what they went through.

When you have to make a choice to move the story ahead,

try to think about what would make one choice better than the other. The reasons we elect one option over another are called "values." We use them every day, and so did people in other times. Ask yourself: What values would the hero of the book have used to make choices? Are those values the same as yours? If they are not, what has happened since that time to make this difference?

But, remember, people are still pretty much the same as they always were. They wanted the same things that we want (security, hope, love, food, shelter, a sense of importance, etc.), and they made their choices to secure these goals.

When you get to the end of one story, try going back and making some different choices. You may be surprised to find out how those choices affect the outcome. Human choice does make a lot of difference in how history turns out. We are not robots, just acting in a play written by someone else. We are people who make decisions, sometimes for good reasons and sometimes not, and our choices really do count.

Most of all, I hope you have a great deal of fun and excitement as you make your choices and move through the history described in these pages.

Kenneth D. Roseman
Rabbi, Temple Shalom
Dallas, Texas

Legend:
All words in **bold** can be found on a map or in the glossary.

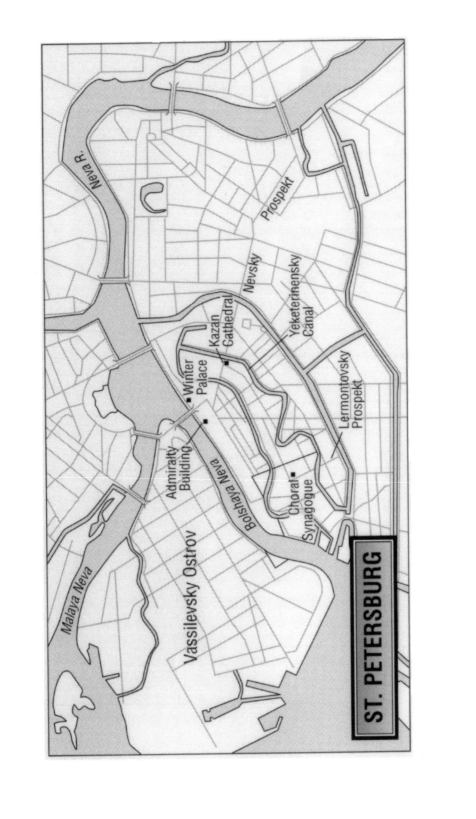

Neva R.

Prospekt

Nevsky

Kazan
Cathedral

Yeketerinensky
Canal

Winter
Palace

Lermontovsky
Prospekt

Admiralty
Building

Malaya Neva

Bolshaya Neva

Choral
Synagogue

Vassilevsky Ostrov

ST. PETERSBURG

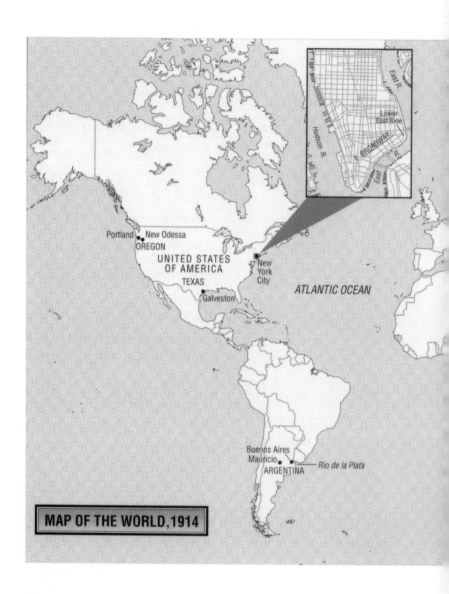

MAP OF THE WORLD, 1914

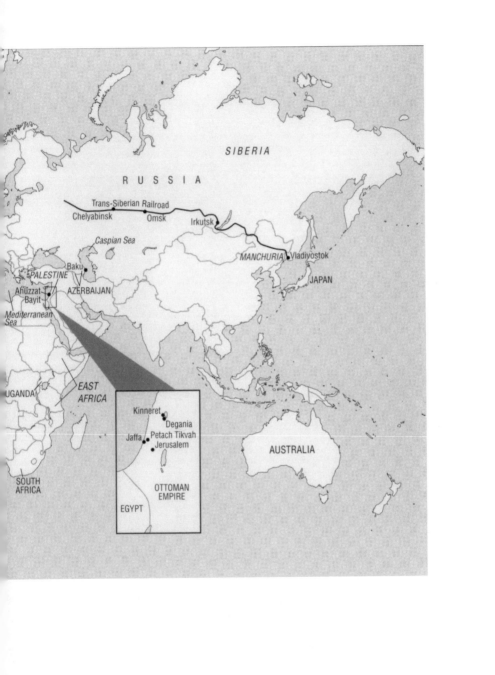

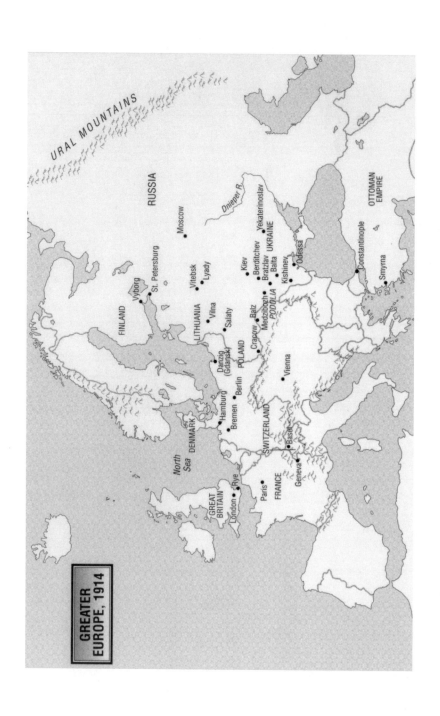

GREATER
EUROPE, 1914

1

It is evening, and the still-bright rays of the sun cast long shadows in the vegetable garden that you and your brother and sister planted as soon as the April frost was gone. Now, the carrots and onions have grown tall, and leafy potato plants with small white blossoms fill the rows.

Most of the harvest you will save in the cold cellar under the house so that your family can eat during the winter. The rest of it Mama will take into the village and sell to non-Jews. As she says, "Even if they hate us—and they do—they still have to eat. And if they're going to pay someone for vegetables, it might as well be us!"

2

There have been many years in your *shtetl* when it wasn't so bad being a Jew, but that has begun to change. A little more than a year ago, terrorists threw a bomb under the carriage of Tzar Alexander II as he crossed a canal bridge in **St. Petersburg,** and he was killed. His son, **Alexander III**, became the new ruler, and he was much less friendly to the Jews than his father. Many of the laws that had given Jews some freedom were abandoned, and Count Ignatiev, the minister of the interior, has now issued the **May Laws** (so named because they first appeared in May 1882). This new series of rules restricts where Jews can live, when they can move from place to place, and whether they can rent property. It looks like your family will have to move from its small village into a larger city.

3

The door of your small house opens, and Mama calls you in for supper. As the five of you sit around the table, your younger sister asks a question. "Papa, why are non-Jews so mean to us?"

You know, of course, what she means. Just last month, some peasants got drunk at Shlomo Moskowitz's tavern and broke all the furniture. They slashed the beard from his face. Then, the mob rushed into the street and destroyed several Jewish businesses. The policemen just stood by and watched— and laughed. Finally, the mob got tired and went home. "Why did they do this?"

"I don't know," says Papa. "It's always been this way in **Russia**. Some years of peace and quiet, then times of violence."

4

"But, Papa," you respond. "Surely there is something else we can do now to make our lives easier and better and safer. What can we do?"

Your father leans back in his chair. "All my life, I have tried to be a good Jew. I studied with the rabbis, and they taught me to listen to the words of Torah. When there were troubles, they said: **Habakkuk** [2:3] is right. 'Though the Messiah be delayed, wait for him.' That's what I think we ought to do now: wait patiently, accept what God gives us, and be good Jews."

You glance at your brother and sister. They, too, are not sure that this is the right plan.

If you think that there is something else that you ought to try,
turn to page 5.

If you think that Papa is right, and you should simply wait for the Messiah,
turn to page 6.

5

It is **Shabbos**, but this day of rest will not turn out like all the others. In the synagogue, there are three young men dressed in modern clothes and the flat caps that university students often wear.

As soon as **Ma'ariv** is over and the congregation has chanted the final prayers, they rush to the front of the **shul**. "Brothers and sisters!" they shout. "The world is changing, changing rapidly. You must be part of these changes, or you will be left behind!"

The rabbi and the leaders of the congregation argue with them, but they are insistent. You overhear them talking about new ideas they have discovered at the university and how working Jews are planning to form trade unions in their factories. "It's a revolution," they tell you, "nothing less than a revolution!"

If you think that the right course would be to attend the university that they describe so favorably,
turn to page 16.

If, on the other hand, you would prefer to join the new workers' movement,
turn to page 17.

6

W aiting, of course, does not mean just sitting in a corner in a trance. There are things to do, lots of things.

You *daven* three times each day—morning, afternoon, and night. In between, you study, mostly *Gemara* but sometimes *midrash* or the *Zohar*. On Monday and Thursday, you reread the *parashah* of the week and **Rashi's** commentary. At least one day each week, you fast, praying that the **tzar** will lift the heavy restrictions that have been placed on Jews in his lands.

Being a religious Jew requires a lot of time and effort, but your parents also arrange with the *shadchan* to find you a mate. You remember the prophet Jeremiah who bought a field in Anatoth as a gesture of confidence that God would not abandon the Jewish people in biblical times. Your own children will serve as just such a statement.

Many of the Jews in your **shtetl** *are followers of one* **chasidic** *sect or another. If you decide to join them,*
turn to page 18.

If you choose to stay with the mainstream of **Mitnagdim,**
turn to page 19.

7

The **St. Petersburg** Conservatory of Music is one of the most famous in the world. Every day in the concert hall, there are brilliant recitals as the best students demonstrate what they have learned.

Among these outstanding students are several young Jewish violinists, such as Mischa Elman and Yascha Heifetz. You wonder if you could ever be as good a musician as they are. But you love the music so much that the effort is worthwhile.

Your life is comfortable. You live in a small room on the fifth floor of a building near the school. You have many friends. After your lessons, you stroll together on the **Nevsky Prospekt** and stop at a cafe for coffee. Comfortable, that is, until May 11, 1891, when you hear a terrible piece of news. All but a few of the richest Jews are being expelled from **St. Petersburg**. The **Neva River** has thawed, but there is new ice in the hearts of **Russia**'s rulers.

If you decide to go back to your **shtetl**
to find work,
turn to page 20.

If you think it's time to leave ***Russia,***
turn to page 26.

8

Some of the wealthy Jews of **St. Petersburg** are convinced they will be treated with more respect if Jewish traditions and history are better known. "Every people has its past; we all have folklore and legends. If the Russian leaders understand that we are really like everyone else, they will treat us like everyone else."

A young scholar named **S. An-Ski** is hired to direct the **Jewish Historical Ethnographical Society**. You are engaged to help with his research. Together, you travel through large areas, especially in the **Ukraine**, collecting folklore, tales, stories, traditions, anything that helps describe the way Jewish people live and think. **An-Ski** is determined to create an archive that reflects a real, but positive, image of the Jews in **Russia**.

As you continue your work with the **Jewish Historical Ethnographical Society**, you have doubts about its effect on the conditions under which Jews live.

If you think you ought to enter politics,
turn to page 31.

If you decide that a business career
would be better,
turn to page 21.

9

Musicians... artists... talkers... thinkers... *luftmenschen* (airheads). The university is full of such people, but what do they really accomplish? A cultural career would be fun, but you can't see a true future for yourself. How would you earn a living? How would you support a family?

Standing in front of the **Admiralty** buildings on the banks of the **Neva River**, you watch a parade of naval cadets. Suddenly, a thought strikes you. Someone has to sell them their equipment, and that someone will make a profit. Perhaps you can find a job with a firm that provides guns, clothing, and food to the **tzar**'s army and navy.

If that is your choice,
turn to page 32.

On the other hand, you have always been attracted to the intellectual world, and you would hate to leave it completely. Becoming a lawyer might be a good compromise: you would make a good living, and you would still be able to think important and deep thoughts.

If you consider this a better choice,
turn to page 27.

10

A Jewish **socialist** party has been organized for all workers in **Russia, Lithuania,** and **Poland.** When you attend one of the **Bund**'s rallies, you listen to the speaker. Loudly, he tells the crowd: "When all the workers unite—not just Jewish workers, but all workers—we shall have enough power to change our lives. Then, we can gain decent working conditions, fair salaries, and the respect we deserve from the capitalists who now exploit us. That's what the **Bund** is all about. Join us, if you share our mission."

You do share their goals. When you see the starving children of Jewish factory workers, you are driven by some internal force to do something, to make a difference. The **Bund** seems like an organization that might help.

If you go to **Shabbos** *services the next week and hear something that surprises you,*
turn to page 22.

If you get into an argument with some people on the street as to whether joining the **Bund** *is a good decision,*
turn to page 33.

11

You join the **Social Democratic Workers' Party** because you are convinced that it will be the key political force in the downfall of tzarism. Its leaders, **Lenin** and **Martov** and others, preach that the working class must seize control of the country before there can be full freedom.

And what are you supposed to do? You have gone to the university. But **Lenin** teaches that educated people must lead the proletariat, the workers, in changing Russian society. Now you must carry the message of the **Social Democratic Workers' Party** into the workplace. By raising the consciousness of the workers about their unhappiness and teaching them how to organize, you will help them lead the revolution. This, **Lenin** assures you, is of critical importance.

And, he casually reminds you, when the revolution comes, Jews, too, will gain their freedom. "By yourselves, you have nothing; with the workers, everything is possible."

*If you choose to go to **Moscow** to find a job among the Jewish workers in a textile plant, turn to page 28.*

If you decide to do your organizing among workers, whether they are Jewish or not, turn to page 23.

12

The **Sadeger** *Rebbe* lives in a style that amazes you. His residence is like a palace, and his chair is a throne with attendants hovering around in the same way that ministers attend the **tzar**. "What's this all about?" you ask.

"We live in the days just before the coming of the Messiah," one of his **Chasidim** whispers to you. "The *rebbe* is teaching us how the heavenly court and the throne of the Holy One appear, what it will be like in that sacred future time. Thanks to our wonderful *rebbe*, we can now go beyond the awful times in which we live and experience the glories of the rule of the Messiah."

If the splendor of this regal court attracts you,
turn to page 34.

If, on the other hand, the difference between how
the **rebbe** *lives and the miserable lives of*
average Jews bothers you,
turn to page 29.

13

You hear that there is a very influential teacher in the *yeshivot* of **Vilna**. **Israel Lipkin**, also known as **Salanter**, has begun a movement to lead Jews toward strict ethical behavior. The **Musar movement** holds that the troubles falling upon the Jews are the result of their own moral shortcomings. If we would only act in accordance with the highest standards of the *halachah* and live by the fear of God, our lives would be far better.

You wonder if **Salanter** is completely right. Maybe the Russians simply hate us; maybe it's not our fault, and he's just blaming the victims for the acts of mean and ugly people.

Yet there is something very attractive in what he says, and would it hurt so much, anyway, if Jews lived a more ethical and moral life? You think that your life would have great meaning if you spent your days teaching his ideas.

If you decide to commit to a career of teaching among the young women of your people, turn to page 24.

If the lessons inspire you to look again at your own life, turn to page 35.

14

Your first impression was correct. **Rabbi Isaac Jacob Reines** is, perhaps, the most passionate man you have ever met. He tells—almost screams at you—his plan for a new kind of *yeshivah*, a place where young Jews can still study the **Talmud**, but where they can also learn modern, secular subjects like mathematics and science. "Our young people need this combination of learning if they are to compete effectively in the modern world without losing their Jewish loyalty. Jews must enter the modern world, but with a firm attachment to their age-old traditions."

Even though **Reines** is absolutely **Orthodox**, his traditional colleagues attack him bitterly. "It is a sin," they boil, "to study anything but Jewish wisdom. To learn secular subjects leads to the devil."

*If you think **Reines's Orthodox** critics may be right, but you are willing to try his ideas, turn to page 30.*

*If you believe **Reines** is on the right track, but it leads in a surprising direction, turn to page 25.*

15

You probably shouldn't have been, but you are surprised when the **tzar** dissolves the **Duma**. He and his advisors simply cannot accept that others might have some voice in how to run the country, that others might want to share his power.

You and many other members of the **Duma** flee across the border of **Finland** to the city of **Vyborg**. There you issue a daring manifesto, declaring that Russians should boycott the government, stop its functioning, and never cease struggling for freedom. The **tzar** is like a modern pharaoh. Repeated pleas for freedom have been rejected. Now, the only course is strong action against him.

After a year in exile, you sneak back into **Russia** to meet with a small cell of **Communists**. What you do not know is that their unit has been infiltrated by a spy from the government. You are arrested at once, given a fraudulent trial, and sent to a work camp in **Siberia**. From this prison, you will never be heard of again. But, as your life ebbs away from slave labor and starvation, you continue to believe that your efforts will ultimately end in freedom for the Russian people.

END

16

The only way to enter the world of modern culture and learning is to go to the university in **St. Petersburg**. Your father reluctantly permits you to enroll, since he realizes that you would probably run away if he refused permission.

When you arrive in **St. Petersburg**, you are awed by the wide **prospekts** and elegant, pastel-colored buildings. The city that Peter the Great planned so carefully 160 years ago is beautiful.

After a year of basic studies at the university, you stop to evaluate what you are doing. You sit in a park on the banks of the **Neva River**. Behind you are the yellow and white buildings of the **Admiralty**, the headquarters of the navy Peter began. What path should you follow?

*If you think you might enter the Conservatory
of Music,
turn to page 7.*

*If you accept a well-paying job from a Jewish
leader of the city,
turn to page 8.*

*If you think there is no future for you in the
academic world and you decide to look
for an alternative,
turn to page 9.*

17

Once, Jews lived in *shtetlach* and had a wide variety of jobs. Today, many more Jews live in cities and work in factories. Many are employed as textile weavers, sugar refiners, liquor distillers, and, of course, merchants and peddlers. For most of them, life is extraordinarily difficult. At best, they can afford a scrawny chicken for ***Shabbos*** dinner, and then they cook the bones for soup after **Havdalah**.

Jewish workers suffer terribly. As you walk along the streets through the muddy alleys where they live, you wonder how it is possible for them to survive.

A conflict rages within you. On the one hand, Jews have always believed in the ideal of universal human progress and decency; on the other hand, these workers are exploited, and their lives are far from those prophetic, religious ideals. You sense that the task of your life is to bring them the hope that the ideals might come true for them.

*If you choose to go to **Vilna** to join the **Bund**, turn to page 10.*

*If you prefer to join the **Social Democratic Workers' Party**, turn to page 11.*

18

Much has changed in **Chasidism** since its founder, **Israel ben Eliezer**, known as the **Ba'al Shem Tov**, began this form of Judaism more than 150 years ago. The **Ba'al Shem Tov** wanted to offer Jews more than study, prayer, and fasting; he believed that every Jew could experience religious joy and ecstasy, that these spiritual exaltations were available to even the simplest person.

Now, several generations of leaders later, there are dozens of sects of **Chasidism**. Each of the *rebbes* has stamped his own distinct personality on his group. Becoming a **Chasid** also means that you must choose which of these groups will gain your loyalty.

*The two major groups in your town are the **Sadeger** and the **Salanter Chasidim**. If you choose to ally yourself with the former, turn to page 12.*

If the second group attracts your membership, turn to page 13.

19

"The **Chasidim** are wrong," you conclude. "They follow their *rebbes* so completely." It seems that these leaders are almost idolized, but you know that it is forbidden to think of any person or object as a rival for God.

"**Mitnagdim**, on the other hand, treat their rabbis as human beings. We respect them for their learning, but we are also quick to recognize their failings and faults. Unlike the Chasidim, we do not hesitate to criticize our religious leaders."

You have always admired **Rabbi Yochanan Ha-Sandlar** of **Mishnaic** fame. He combined a trade with continual study of the Jewish tradition. You, too, become a shoemaker. But you also spend an hour or so every morning at the house of study. It gives you great pleasure to master even a small amount of Jewish knowledge every day.

In the corner of the *beit hamidrash*, there is a man who studies intensely. There is a certain aura about this man; you are attracted to him. You decide to approach him.

Turn to page 14.

20

Y ou can hardly believe this nightmare. You and more than 2,000 other Jews are being forced out of this lovely city, pushed back into the towns and cities of the **Pale of Settlement**.

But it's true. You pack your few belongings and prepare to leave. Some Jews resist, but they are arrested, placed in chains, and marched away under military guard.

The trek home is awful. The roads are filled with Jewish refugees, struggling through the sticky spring mud and trying to make some sense of the tragedy that has just happened to them. You know that Russians do not like Jews, but how could they be so cruel and filled with hate?

When you arrive home, your family greets you with hugs and kisses, but you feel just a little bit of "We told you so." That may be the most painful hurt of all.

There is not much work in the **shtetl**. *If you decide to become an apprentice, learning a craft, turn to page 36.*

If you think that Papa may have been right and that you should learn more about your religion, turn to page 47.

21

The most wealthy and powerful Jew in all of **Russia** is **Baron David Gunzberg**. After he made his fortune building most of the Russian railway system, he became a banker and the chief representative of Jewish interests at the **tzar**'s court.

But he is also an intellectual. His library has 52,000 books, and he speaks many languages. The *tzedakah* he distributes, especially in the region of **Podolia**, is legendary.

Your research work for the **Jewish Historical-Ethnographical Society** is useful in Gunzberg's office. He needs people who can go into a region, talk to the local residents, and find answers to questions about new business projects. You do that well.

If you accompany the Baron on a visit to a high government official,
turn to page 56.

If you go on another research trip,
turn to page 38.

22

It's **Shabbos** and of course, you're in **shul**. The **parashah** is *Kedoshim*, a section of Leviticus you've heard many times before. But this time, you hear it in a new way: "Take care of the poor." "Use honest weights and measures." "Pay wages to workers when they are due." "Treat other people as you want to be treated yourself."

Why, these are the same words that the leaders of the **Bund** have been speaking. You had never before realized that they come straight out of the Torah, but, of course, they do. You feel strong and proud to know that Judaism, your tradition, has advocated the rights of workers and economic fairness for thousands of years.

If you find work in a factory yourself, but continue your education at night, turn to page 58.

If you are so moved by the Torah passage you have heard that you decide to take a very different path, turn to page 50.

23

Some Jewish workers have joined the **Osvobozhdenie Truda**, "The Liberation of Labor Party." When you ask them whether they are members because they are Jews, they laugh, even sneer. "There is no Jewish question," they reply. "Only a Russian question. It is the revolution that counts, not being a Jew or anything else. So what if we stop being Jews, as long as we can change this terrible system and bring about democracy?"

These "Trudoviki" challenge you. Is it worth giving up being a Jew to gain a more general goal? Or can you bring about the revolution and still remain a Jew? Some say you can; others think that it is an either/or choice.

*If you agree that you must choose between being Jewish and revolution,
turn to page 60.*

*If you think you can have both,
turn to page 42.*

24

Some young women, like **Puah Rakowski**, have elected to seek a more modern education and to organize Jewish women's societies. But you decide that there are more traditional girls than modern ones and that it would be more effective to teach them in **Orthodox** schools.

A new school has been organized in **Cracow**. It is called **Beis Ya'akov**, and its purpose is to train young Jewish women to become teachers. Then, they will be able to spread learning to many more girls. That sounds like an excellent idea to you, and you gain a position as an instructor in this new academy.

If you are swept up in the power that comes to these students as they gain education,
turn to page 53.

If you discover that education might actually lead to Jewish weakness and you want to halt that trend,
turn to page 44.

25

It is highly unlikely that the Russians will open the doors that lead into the modern world. They won't admit you, and they won't accept you. And, clearly, anti-Semitism persists elsewhere, even in **France**. There is only one way: to create your own nation where you can control the entire society yourselves.

A Jewish journalist from **Vienna**, **Theodore Herzl**, has summoned Jewish leaders representing every shade of **Zionist** opinion. From all over the world, they gather at **Basle** for the **First Zionist Congress**, and you are there, too. **Herzl**'s essay, "Altneuland," speaks of his dream of creating a Jewish state. But, he says, "It is no dream if you will it to happen."

Long and heated debates continue late each night, but everyone is of a similar mind. Somehow, we must find a way to return to the Jewish homeland, to **Zion**.

If you believe this can best be accomplished through a religious organization, turn to page 54.

If you prefer a more secret structure, turn to page 64.

26

This is not like other anti-Semitic actions that you have experienced. Those were local. Now there is a hatred of Jews that extends throughout **Russia**. Nowhere would you be safe and secure. Obviously, there can be no future for you here; you must leave.

Baron Maurice de Hirsch, one of the richest Jews in **Germany**, has founded the **Jewish Colonization Association (ICA)**. Its aim is to help Jews like you escape tzarist **Russia**, its pogroms and its poverty, and resettle in lands of freedom and opportunity.

You go to work for them, and you get great pleasure doing the *mitzvah* of *pikuach nefesh*. To save Jewish lives by helping people leave **Russia** seems like the most important work you can do.

*One day, you are offered the chance to go to overseas as **ICA**'s field representative. If you accept,*

turn to page 55.

*If you think it is more important that you stay in **Russia**,*

turn to page 37.

27

Maxim Vinaver is well known as a lawyer who defends Jewish rights. Together with **Baron Horace Gunzberg** and **Henry Sliosberg**, he went to **Count Witte** to persuade the minister to make life easier for Jews. As you heard it later, **Witte** agreed, provided that Jews would not engage in revolutionary activities. The Baron was prepared to accept this condition, but **Vinaver** would not. "Jews have a right to stand up for their rights, even it means protest," he apparently said.

Vinaver is not friendly to the **Zionists**, because he believes that Jews ought to be able to work out their future in **Russia**. However, he is completely committed to *tzedakah*, to relieving the misery of poor Jews throughout the **tzar's** empire.

*If you choose to work with **Vinaver** in his political activities, turn to page 49.*

If you would prefer to study law with him, turn to page 39.

28

The work in the factory is hard, but that's not important. What counts is the time that you spend with small groups of workers, teaching them about the coming revolution. "You will be the leaders," you tell them. "The bourgeoisie, the army, and the peasants will follow you. But you must be committed to taking power, even by force if necessary. Some of us will die, but all **Russia** will benefit. The sacrifice will be worthwhile."

You missed something rather important while you were talking with these workers. One of them has been taking notes. You thought he was just a very interested student, but he was really a government spy. **Count Viacheslav von Plehve**, the minister of the interior, hasn't been idle. Your revolution won't happen without opposition.

You are arrested and sent to prison.

*If you are exiled to **Siberia**,*
turn to page 51.

If the court sentences you to a prison
*near **Kishinev**,*
turn to page 41.

29

On *Shabbos*, the **rebbe** enters a large room and sits on a gold-painted chair that looks to you like a throne. He wears a black **kittel** of expensive fabric, gold threads weave through his **tallis**, and his **streimel** is adorned with the finest mink fur. He appears like the most powerful *boyar* of the region, and his disciples show him the same respect that the peasants show to the lord of the local manor.

Something about this picture troubles you. Yes, of course it is important that the **rebbe** behave in ways that will gain him respect; he is a very influential man. But the Judaism that you believe in tells you that it is more worthwhile to use your wealth to care for the less-fortunate people in society. After all, the Torah teaches that you were "a slave in the land of Egypt" and that you now have a special responsibility to others who are "enslaved."

If you look for a leader who is more spiritual in his approach,
turn to page 43.

If you are turned off by religion and seek strength in national unity,
turn to page 62.

30

A few years with **Reines** and you realize that you must have a university education if you are to succeed in the modern world. Apparently, his critics were right when they said that his way would lead to even more non-Jewish study.

But you believe firmly that you must learn modern history and science to be a full part of the emerging modern world. Judaism will die if it does not change, and you love your Jewish identity too much to let that happen. Modernization and change are not disloyalty; quite the contrary, they are the way to save the Jewish future. A person involved in the *Haskalah* may be very rational, but he or she can still also be religious—just in a different way.

As you continue both your university studies and your Jewish involvement, you become aware that some of your fellow students express themselves best through the arts, while others choose a more political path.

If you prefer an artistic life,
turn to page 63.

If you find a career in politics more appealing,
turn to page 46.

31

The thunderbolt of expulsion from **St. Petersburg** struck quickly. Almost overnight, most of the Jews who live in the capital are forced to leave for the **Pale of Settlement**. You are allowed to remain in the city, protected as you are by a *shtadlan*, a rich Jew who is like an ambassador of the Jews to the Russian leadership.

Henry Sliosberg, sometimes called "the attorney for the Jews," suggests you join the **Constitutional Democratic Party**. "We call ourselves **Kadets**," he tells you. "We love **Russia**, but we also want more Jewish rights and more liberal policies from the **tzar**."

Sliosberg often refers to the prophets of the Bible. "They wanted justice for everyone," he proclaims. "We must fight for that ideal." But his fight seems more for the rights of the rich members of the **Kadet** party, and this bothers you.

If you think that you would do more good helping real working Jews, turn to page 22.

On the other hand, if you think that you can make more of a difference if you have access to highly placed Russian leaders, turn to page 48.

32

Your idea is a good one; the **tzar's** forces need supplies. If you can figure out what to sell, you might do very well.

There is a Jewish chemist named **Chaim Weizmann**. He has invented some kind of gunpowder that is supposed to be much better than the one that is being used right now. You convince **Weizmann** to let you try to interest the Russian navy in his discovery. "After all," you tell him, "this will probably be your best chance for lasting fame. If your gunpowder is really so great, the world will remember your name forever."

Weizmann smiles and tells you to go ahead. The smile puzzles you, and you remember it for a long time. But you can't eat a smile, so you begin visiting naval commanders.

*One of them tells you that there is a military testing base in the **Ural Mountains**. If you went there, you might succeed. To pursue that choice, turn to page 57.*

Most of the time, however, the officers will not see you unless you offer them substantial bribes. If that causes you to reconsider your career, turn to page 65.

33

A **Chasid** on the street confronts you. "Ha!" he sniffs. "You think you can bring the Messiah by working in a factory? *Moshiach* will come because Jews pray and study and fast in the synagogue. That's the only way."

You are just about to answer him when a striking man steps between the two of you. "Idiot!" he hisses. "We shall bring the Messiah into the midst of the Jewish nation when we make Jews productive members of the modern economy. Too many Jews are middle-class, parasites earning their living from the work of others. We must create a class of Jewish workers who create things, and then the Messiah—if there is even such a thing—will appear."

Later, this passionate man introduces himself as
Chaim Zhitlowsky. *If you think that you ought to learn more about his teaching,*
turn to page 40.

On the other hand, if you think that Jews cannot depend on the greater Russian economy but must take care of themselves,
turn to page 59.

34

Y ou may try to escape the true ugliness of Russian Jewish life at the *rebbe*'s court, but you can't. **Chasidim** doesn't protect you from the harsh realities of Russian society. Just before Russian Easter, a dangerous time in Jewish life, priests remind the faithful of how biblical Jews rejected Jesus as the Christ and how their modern descendants are equally to be despised. Some of the worshippers take such messages seriously and attack Jews.

This year is especially bad. The Russian military have been badly defeated by the Japanese in 1905. The government and the church blame the disaster on the Jews; scapegoating encourages people to forget the real causes of their frustrations.

All it takes is a forged document, **The Protocols of the Elders of Zion**, which the **Okhrana** published in **France**. It tells of how Jews want to control the world, and many Russians believe it. Pogroms break out in many cities and towns.

If you write an article describing what a pogrom is like,
turn to page 52.

If you hide, waiting for the attacks to cease,
turn to page 61.

35

Rabbi **Salanter** inspired you to return to the source of all Jewish wisdom, the **Tanach**. It was there, reading and rereading the Book of Psalms, that you came across a verse that changed your life: "When you eat from the labor of your own hands, you shall be happy" (128:2).

You listen to your own **musar**, to the ethical teaching of this biblical wisdom. Only a person, you believe, who has earned his or her own income, whose work is productive, and whose life adds to the value of society, only such a person can find true happiness.

You realize that you must find such constructive work. But where?

If you look for your occupation in agriculture, turn to page 45.

If you think carrying your message into a factory would suit you better, turn to page 11.

36

Soon you realize that you can become a tailor, a carpenter, a leather worker, a tinsmith… you can train to be whatever you want and you will still not be able to earn enough money to live a decent life. There simply are no good jobs. All your training will only permit you to starve to death with a craft!

There must be some way, you think to yourself, to live with the dignity that is due a Jewish worker, some way to earn a fair living, to have some control over the conditions in which you work.

*If you decide to look for a Jewish labor union,
turn to page 66.*

*If your thinking is interrupted by the outbreak of
World War I and you decide to join the
Russian army,
turn to page 86.*

37

All around you, you see signs of disaster. Men who used to have good jobs now cannot find even the most ordinary work. Children walk through the streets without shoes, without coats, their clothing torn and filthy. The **May Laws** have forced proud Jews to survive only on *tzedakah*, and some of them cannot bring themselves to do so.

Desperation leads some men to desert their wives and children. Others go to **America**, **Argentina**, **South Africa**, **England**, or **Australia** with your help, hoping to build new lives and later send for their families. Occasionally, a man gives up, simply turns to the wall, and dies. What a tragedy has come upon your people!

If you commit your life to easing the pain that has afflicted the Jews of the Pale of Settlement, turn to page 108.

If, however, you are afraid that you will be caught up in these destructive forces, turn to page 68.

38

Baron **David Gunzberg** sends you all the way to **Odessa**, a railroad journey of over a thousand miles. "This is big," he tells you. "We could win the contract for all of the rail lines and stations in southern **Ukraine**."

As your train snakes southward in late March, you listen to the conversation of two Russian priests who sit opposite you. "Easter is approaching," one says, "the time when those cursed Jews killed Christ. It is time for our people to take revenge. This Sunday, I will encourage them to visit God's anger on the nonbelievers."

When they leave the train at **Berditchev**, you make a fast decision and hop off, too. You must warn the Jews of this town that bad things are going to happen. How ironic it is that you learned about an upcoming pogrom on a railroad that the Baron, a Jew, had built.

*If you encourage the Jews of **Berditchev** to find another future,*
turn to page 69.

If you think that they can protect themselves,
turn to page 111.

39

Law school makes sense. Lawyers are respected and make a good living. It is a career you could not have imagined when you were living with your parents in the *shtetl*.

There is only one problem. A Jew may not practice law without special permission from the minister of justice. And this official is a notorious anti-Semite. "More Jewish lawyers," he sniffs. "We have too many of those parasites already. All they are good for is stirring up trouble."

Even if you were to study privately with **Vinaver** or one of the other prominent Jewish lawyers, you could not practice. What would be the use?

You consider joining some other students on the street to protest this unfair restriction of your right to choose a career. If this is what you do, turn to page 92.

If, on the other hand, you think that there is no future and that you must leave the country, turn to page 72.

40

Russia is changing. Once, there was only the **tzar** and his government. Now, some political parties are beginning to emerge, and you are faced with several choices. Should you affiliate with one party or another? With any party at all?

Chaim Zhitlowsky teaches you that the improvement of life for Jews must go hand in hand with the renewal of all Russians. To do that, the Jews must ally themselves with the **Socialist Revolutionary Party**. The Socialist Revolutionaries want to forge a close alliance with other radical groups to support teams of workers who would bargain with employers as a group and redistribute large landholdings to the peasants.

Changing the relationship of workers and bosses so extensively will not be popular. You expect some opposition, but you are unprepared for its strength. You have failed to understand how strongly the upper class will protect its privileges.

If you react to this resistance by taking to the streets in protest,
turn to page 94.

If you respond with less of a confrontation,
turn to page 115.

41

While you are in prison, you hear rumors of a massive pogrom in **Kishinev**, and this makes you more afraid even than being inside this dark and damp prison. "If they can massacre Jews in the streets, they can certainly kill me in here. I've got to find a way to escape."

You smuggle a letter out by bribing one of the guards. He gives it to some traveling Jewish merchants, who carry it first to **Constantinople** and then to **Smyrna**. The Jewish community there has a long history of performing a special *mitzvah*: *pidyon shevu'im*, ransoming the captives.

You don't know exactly how it was done, but somehow they arranged your release. You assume a lot of money changed hands, and you hope that someday you will be able to repay this generosity. But first, you must decide what to do with the rest of your life.

If you decide that it's important to tell your story to other Jews,
turn to page 75.

If you just want to find safety in a large city where no one will know you,
turn to page 116.

42

All the calls for revolution have sparked a different kind of protest. Russian **Cossacks**, peasants, and workers in the **Ukraine** are all convinced that Jew-oppressors are responsible for all the troubles of their lives. "Jews collect the taxes; Jews keep us poor; Jews cheat us when we go to the tavern to buy vodka … everywhere we turn, we find Jews. Let's teach them a real lesson."

Anti-Semitic groups like the **Black Hundreds** and **Narodnaya Volya** incite the mob to action. On April 6, 1903, they strike in the city of **Kishinev** and in many other towns. The pogrom is carefully planned, even though the government's role is artfully concealed. More than fifty Jews are killed and hundreds are seriously wounded in **Kishinev** alone.

If you are so angered by these attacks that you determine to take strong action,
turn to page 98.

If you think a more diplomatic approach would be preferable,
turn to page 117.

43

You become impressed with the ideas of **Asher Ginsberg**, who is better known by his pen name of **Ahad Ha-Am**. As early as 1889, he wrote that *lo zot haderech*, "this is not the right way." The kind of Jewish religion practiced in **Russia**, he argued, would not provide spiritual guidance for Jews. Their valuescould only be realized when Jews had a national center that could lead to a collective ethical and moral code. Only the building up of a Jewish national home in **Palestine**, **Ahad Ha-Am** has written, will stimulate Jewish culture and life.

In **Odessa**, he has founded a group called **Bnai Moshe** to promote his ideas. You travel to that southern Russian city and enlist in his group.

If you find that it leads you in exactly the right direction,
continue on page 100.

If, however, an event occurs that shocks you so deeply that you change your path,
turn to page 79.

44

Contact with the modern world can be dangerous; *Haskalah* can convince Jews to leave Judaism behind in favor of what they imagine are more attractive ways of living. But reading a newspaper or joining a political party should not cause Jews to abandon their precious heritage.

You enlist in a group founded by the Rabbi of **Belz, Joshua Rokeach.** It is called Machzikei Da'at, "Upholders of the Faith," and its goal is to use the same instruments that could weaken Judaism to strengthen it. The newspaper it publishes teaches people how to follow traditional Jewish ways and yet also be part of today's world.

All of the sainted rabbi's teaching, however, will not make Russian peasants love Jews. After a particularly violent pogrom in your *shtetl* of **Belz,** bloodied and exhausted survivors gather at the *shul.* "What are we supposed to do next?" you wonder. "And if we do not act courageously now, when?"

*If the trauma of the pogrom shakes your faith
and you take a radical path,
turn to page 81.*

*If you try to persuade others to adopt
traditional ways,
turn to page 121.*

45

"**J**ews must follow their religion," the man with the huge white beard and high bald forehead asserts forcefully. "But the religion that has kept us in *yeshivot* and synagogues is not our true faith. What we must do is return to a life touched by the natural world, an existence in which we must till the fields and work the land."

Aaron David Gordon, the advocate of the "Religion of Labor," has become your hero. He speaks of the dignity of common toil and the religious meaning of hard work. "Only by the sweat of our brows," Gordon says, "will we purify Jewish life."

He plans to move to **Deganiah**, to a pioneering settlement in **Palestine**, where he will put his ideas into practice. He calls his beliefs "Labor Zionism," by which he means that you will build up the Holy Land by physical labor.

*If you follow **Gordon** to **Palestine** to act on his philosophy,*
turn to page 102.

*If you stay in **Russia** and try to organize the working class,*
turn to page 82.

46

Politics, the art of convincing other people to do something, to make change happen, to improve the conditions of life for Jews ... wait a minute! For Jews alone? Why not for every person who lives in **Russia**? Why should you limit your efforts only to your own people? But wait again. Only Jews are oppressed and persecuted by the **tzar**. They need your work more than other people. Why not concentrate on those who are the most desperate and the most in need of assistance?

The choice is difficult. All people are deserving of help, but, perhaps, some are more deserving than others. It's a dilemma, and you're not quite sure how you will respond.

If you choose to concentrate your political work among Jews,
turn to page 83.

You learn of a new leader who will guide you to reach out to a broader group and help more people. If this approach attracts you,
turn to page 123.

47

Back home, you spend most of every day studying and praying in the *shul*. You listen to the older men as they discuss and debate serious questions of life. In the street outside the *shul*, others speak of these men with disrespect. *Luftmenschen*, they call them, "airheads." But you find their conversations important, and soon you find yourself joining in.

Papa must have been right all along. Non-Jewish Russians will never accept us. All we can do is let time pass, honor our religion, and do *mitzvot* for one another. If we are faithful to the Holy One, Blessed be He, the Messiah will surely come.

One day, a strange young man **davens** *next to you in the synagogue. He tells you he is a* **Chasid***, a follower of* **Rabbi Shneur Zalman** *of* **Lyady***, founder of* **Chabad***. He speaks of his way of thinking with such enthusiasm that you are immediately drawn to him. If you choose to follow* **Chabad***,*
turn to page 106.

On the other hand, if you believe that the Messiah will first appear in **Jerusalem** *and you want to be there to greet him,*
turn to page 67.

48

The **Kadets** believe that change will happen slowly, in an orderly and legal fashion. At first, you share their optimism. But one day, you overhear a conversation outside the office of **Constantine Pobedonostsev**. The Overprocurator of the Holy Synod, the highest spiritual advisor to **Tzar Alexander III**, believes that Jews are the cause of all **Russia**'s problems and that they must be eliminated, by death, if necessary, or certainly by forcing many Jews to leave.

If such a high-ranking official thinks that this is the solution to what he calls "**Russia**'s Jewish problem," then the **Kadets** are wrong. But what to do?

One solution is to warn Jews of the threat. Perhaps they can find ways to protect themselves. If this is the path you choose, turn to page 88.

One solution is to warn Jews of the threat. Perhaps they can find ways to protect themselves. If this is the path you choose, turn to page 88.

*If **Pobedonostsev**'s plans throw you into confusion and despair and you begin to think that there is no future for Jews in **Russia**, turn to page 109.*

*If **Pobedonostsev**'s plans throw you into confusion and despair and you begin to think that there is no future for Jews in **Russia**, turn to page 109.*

49

Frustration increases. **Tzar Nicholas II** seems unable to understand how angry most Russians—not just Jews—are. Finally, in early October 1905, the railroad workers strike. And when the trains stop running, the country stops running.

The **tzar** is forced to proclaim a constitution on October 17 and to call a **Duma**, a parliament, into session. But only six months later, he issues a decree that makes the **Duma** powerless. The little authority that it was supposed to have has been stripped away from it.

Across **Russia** there is rage. And among Jews, who had hoped that the **Duma** would be a vehicle for gaining and protecting their rights, sadness reigns.

*If you abandon **Vinaver** and the political work in the **Duma** that you were doing with him,*
turn to page 91.

If you believe that this is only a temporary setback,
turn to page 113.

50

As you become increasingly aware of the religious roots of your ideals, you know that you must follow that path. But most Jews of **Russia** are **Orthodox**, and most **Orthodox** Jews of your time are preoccupied with the observance of ritual *mitzvot: kashrut, Shabbos,* the laws of the **Talmud** and the *Shulchan Aruch.* They don't know what you are talking about when you stand up in the **yeshivah** and try to discuss social justice.

One day, while you are supposed to be studying a *daf gemora* from tractate *Gittin*, you discover a tattered, yellowed old journal entitled *Tevunah*. Most of the articles appear to deal with how rabbinic *halachah* relates to ethical social issues.

If this journal intrigues you and you read further, turn to page 114.

If, however, you come to the conclusion that rabbinic Judaism is irrelevant to your deepest concerns, turn to page 73.

51

Y ou are transported in chains, first on the train, then walking miles, until you arrive at the prison camp in Yakutsk. There, you are put to backbreaking work in a gold mine, extracting the ore that will be used to make jewelry for the beautiful women of the despised ruling class. Even more than being in prison, you hate helping them adorn their luxurious lives when so many Russians exist in utter poverty.

Naturally, there are no Jews in Yakutsk, and so, gradually, over the years, you lose touch with your Jewish roots. You cannot remember when the holy days are, even how to celebrate. **Yiddish** sounds foreign to you; all you speak is Russian.

In 1905, **Nicholas II** is forced to create the first **Duma**. This first attempt at democracy in **Russia** has little real power, but it does act to declare amnesty for political prisoners, and you are released.

Turn to page 96.

52

A Hebrew-language newspaper, *Ha-Yom*, which is published in **St. Petersburg**, sends you a message. They want you to write a firsthand account of the pogrom. It's a challenge you cannot pass up.

You slip out of your hiding place and move through the town, making mental notes of what you see. And what you see horrifies you. Virtually every building in the Jewish section of town has been devastated; the glass windows are shattered, and some are on fire. Inside, the merchandise has been ransacked and stolen.

In one house, you find a weeping woman, her hands covered with blood. "I tried to save my husband and children, but the mob beat them to death." Elsewhere, injured Jews begin to bind up their wounds. The disaster is widespread; everyone has suffered. You find it hard to put such horrors down on paper, but you do, and you send your account off to the editor.

If you conclude from this pogrom that Jews must change the system,
turn to page 77.

If you think that your article will enflame non-Jewish public opinion,
turn to page 99.

53

Educated Jewish women cannot be held back. Once they become aware of the possibilities that life can offer them, they demand new opportunities. Some of your students organize a new women's group called **Bnos Tzion**, a Jewish women's federation in **Poland**. Others become fervent **Zionists** and work to build up the land of **Palestine**.

Whatever their different interests, however, they all share a common cause. When World War I breaks out, young Jewish men serve in the Russian army, and some of them are wounded. The women are outraged to learn that these casualties will not be treated in Russian military hospitals, that they are forced to travel back to the **Pale of Settlement** for medical care. Jewish women unite to nurse them back to health.

If you find yourself in a heated argument in the wards of a new Jewish hospital, turn to page 120.

If you meet a very special Jewish patient, turn to page 101.

54

When you return from the **First Zionist Congress**, **Rabbi Reines** meets you at the railroad depot. "What happened?" he asks excitedly. And you tell him that there is now a worldwide **Zionist** organization, dedicated to making **Palestine** into a modern Jewish homeland.

Reines virtually leaps up and down. "They are right! The pain and the suffering of our people in **Russia** can only be lessened if they can move to a country where Jews control the government. Only there will our people be free from pogroms."

Together, you organize **Orthodox** Jewish **Zionists** into a group called **Mizrachi**. "We have not forgotten you, **Jerusalem**," says your poster, echoing the words of the psalm (137:5). "We shall return, and we shall rekindle a Jewish religious center in the holy city."

But the Russian government has other ideas. Soon, they outlaw your group and all **Zionist** activities. They think you are traitors, disloyal to **Russia**.

If you decide to take a more political approach, turn to page 104.

If you react out of anger, turn to page 84.

55

Thousands of Jews leave **Russia** every month. Most of them come to **St. Petersburg**, then take a ship to **Bremen** or **Hamburg** and then another ship for the long journey to America or some other destination.

At the dock, there are tearful farewells. You know that most of these emigrants will never see their families again. Even writing a letter will be difficult; perhaps they will communicate only once a year. What courage it must take for them take such a huge step, to go to a land where they do not know the language, the customs, the people. They will be very much alone in the New World, but you have determined to join them, to help them settle in their new homes. That, too, will be a considerable *mitzvah*.

*If you decide that the best choice is for you to go to **Argentina**, where the **Jewish Colonization Association (ICA)** is helping many people build new lives,*
turn to page 107.

*If you elect to join the travelers who will reach **Galveston, Texas**,*
turn to page 87.

56

When **Baron David Gunzberg** goes to meet with the minister of finance, he asks you to accompany him. "You've seen what it's like in the countryside. You can help him understand the real situation of our people. You can show him that if Jews are ruined, there will be economic disaster in other sectors of society."

But the minister isn't interested in listening. He charges that Jews own distilleries and saloons. They get the peasants and workers drunk every week, and all the evils of society come from this Jewish plot to cheat honest Russians of their money.

Gunzberg later explains to you that this outburst was mostly for show. What the minister really fears is Jewish competitors who will do better than Christians. One way or another, however, you sense that Jews will have a bad time. That is confirmed when the Baron is forced to resign as a member of the **St. Petersburg** city council. No Jews may any longer hold such a high public office.

*If you fall into deep despair,
turn to page 89.*

*If you think things will get better,
turn to page 110.*

57

You journey to **Moscow** and then nearly another thousand miles on the railroad until you do, in fact, come to such a military base. But what interests you is not the testing of gunpowder.

What you discover is a group of young Jewish teenagers. They tell you that they were taken from their families by force, snatched in the middle of the night, and sent far away to serve in the army for twenty-five years. The stories they tell you are awful. They have been beaten, starved, called horrible names, forced to work day after day with little sleep. It's nothing less than torture, all because they are Jews.

One night, as you lie quietly in your room, you wonder if you could help these Jewish soldier-captives to escape. If you think this is what you should do,
turn to page 90.

If, on the other hand, you decide to stay at the base and teach both Jewish and non-Jewish soldiers that there is an alternative,
turn to page 70.

58

A member of the **Bund**, you think, who is not a worker is somehow a fraud. You cannot allow yourself to feel like a fake, so you find work in the Morozov textile factory in **Moscow**. There, from early morning until late evening, you push cartloads of fabric from the looms to the packing room. It's very hard work, and you are paid only a small wage. But, at least, you are a true worker.

At night, you listen to a **Bund** organizer who has journeyed to **Moscow** from **Odessa**. He is full of optimism and good news. He continues to teach you, but now a different "Torah," the Torah of the worker. And you learn. You learn that the workers of **Odessa** are organized. Recently, they have declared a strike. The owner of the factory has had to give in to their demands. Now, they work only ten hours each day, and they have *Shabbos* off. This is a real victory. And you can do the same.

*The **Bund** organizer also tells you about a pogrom that may happen in **Berditchev** and how Jewish workers are prepared to fight off the mob. If you are moved by this story, turn to page 111.*

If, however, you feel a need to tell the Bund's story to many people, turn to page 93.

59

The island of **Vassilevsky Ostrov** lies across the **Neva River** from **St. Petersburg**. You like to sit in front of the university and look at the capital city, its pastel-colored buildings glowing gently in the muted sun of the White Nights. But tonight, you are restless, so you wander into a bookstore and begin to browse.

A little book almost jumps off the shelf into your hand: *Auto-Emancipation* by **Leon Pinsker**. You start to read, and what you find changes your life. **Pinsker** demands that Jews take responsibility for their own future. "No other power will care for us; we must be for ourselves. We must prepare to govern ourselves in our own land. Jews must live a normal life like every other people."

What **Pinsker** says sounds absolutely right to you. You've seen too much anti-Semitism in **Russia** to trust anyone else to care for your welfare. The only question is: What to do?

*One choice is to emigrate to **America**. To do that, turn to page 74.*

*Or, you can work with a Russian group that has adopted **Pinsker**'s ideas. To do that, turn to page 95.*

60

Back in 1874, one of the true leaders of the **Osvobozhdenie Truda** had fled to **Berlin**. Now, **Pavel Axelrod** lives in **Geneva**, where he and several others edit the organization's newspaper, *Iskra*, "The Spark." What they hope is that their words will light the fire of revolution, even from as far away as **Switzerland**.

You join **Axelrod** and work with him and other leaders of the **Social Democratic Workers' Party**. Your articles are aimed especially at university students in **Russia**, because you expect that they will become the core of a group of teachers. In factories and villages, in army and navy bases, in restaurants and marketplaces, they will spread the message and create a mass movement, a radical group whose demands for change will be irresistible.

*If you continue your work outside **Russia**, fearing arrest if you were to return, turn to page 97.*

If you cannot stay away and choose to go back, turn to page 76.

61

"Arise and go now to the city of slaughter… Behold…the spattered blood… of the dead… On wreckage doubly wrecked, scroll heaped on manuscript, fragments again fragmented—pause not upon this havoc; go your way… Wherefore, O Lord, and why? It is a silence only God can bear."

A poem by a young Russian Jewish poet, **Chayyim Nachman Bialik**. But what a poem! Its depiction of the horrors of the pogrom strikes deep into your heart; its images penetrate into your very soul. You lie awake at night, staring straight at the ceiling, imprisoned by the poet's words no less than if you had been chained in a solitary jailhouse cell. You cannot escape.

You now recognize that there can be no honor and no glory living in *galut*, in exile from the sacred presence that dwells in the holy, promised land.

Some advise you to seek counsel from the rabbi of the **shul** *down the street. If you do, turn to page 118.*

If you join a **Zionist** *youth group, turn to page 78.*

62

Admitting that religion may not be the answer is not easy for you; it's a little like rejecting your parents. To push you into a better mood, some of your friends invite you to a party. You go reluctantly, but maybe they are right and it's time to move ahead.

"What a special people we are," the young scholar says. He stands in a group in the corner of the tavern where the party is being held and speaks forcefully. "Jews are a nation. We express our ideals like any other nation, through the life of people. And what is most important is that we must develop a Jewish will to live at the very highest level possible. We must demonstrate to the world that our history has led us to be not just a nation like any other, but a spiritual nation. That will be our lasting glory."

"Who is he?" you ask. "**Dubnow**" is the reply. "**Shimon Dubnow**. He has become the most famous interpreter of the Jewish people's history in our time. You should get to know him."

*If **Dubnow**'s ideas lead you into a political life, turn to page 119.*

If you follow him in his career as an educator, turn to page 80.

63

In the **beit hamidrash**, you loved the stories that the rabbis told. When you read the *Agadah*, the tales of ancient rabbis, fables about animals that could talk and accounts of miraculous events always captured your imagination. Perhaps you could tell the stories of your time. The life of a writer attracts you as a way of teaching modern truths to the next generation.

If this is the path you choose,
turn to page 122.

You're still thinking about this choice as you walk down the street. A young man is sitting on a stool, painting a portrait of a pretty girl. What a beautiful image he is creating! It would be wonderful to be the source of such beauty and joy in the life of other people.

You realize that the second commandment forbids the creation of "graven images." But that, you argue with yourself, means sculpture. It doesn't say "painted images," so that must be permitted.

If you think that you could become a good
painter,
turn to page 103.

64

Only in tiny, secret cells can the **Zionist** movement continue, now that the Russian government has made it so clear that they consider you traitors. But you are convinced that your work is even more important than ever. Vicious pogroms and anti-Semitic laws have made it increasingly difficult to live as a Jew. The right solution is to find a refuge for tortured, oppressed Jews.

The British government is appalled at the violence directed at the Jews of **Russia**. When **Zionist** leaders appeal for their help, they offer a plan. They will dedicate part of their **East African** colony, **Uganda**, as a safe haven for Jews. **Palestine** is not available, they tell you, because its Turkish rulers will not allow large-scale Jewish settlement. But **Uganda** is a real possibility.

If you think that this is a good idea,
turn to page 105.

If you cannot support the plan and choose a
different kind of action,
turn to page 85.

65

This kind of corruption offends you. All your life, you have read that the person acceptable to God is one who never takes bribes (Ps. 15:5). And here it is that everyone assumes that the only way to do business is to engage in such unethical behavior.

The more you try to do the right thing, the less you think that the system can ever be fixed. Reform is not the answer; it's too broken to repair with gradual changes.

You really have a simple choice: either accept society as it is or overthrow the system.

If you compromise your principles and decide to do business the way everyone else does, turn to page 112.

If you will not pay a bribe and conclude that major, radical change is needed, turn to page 71.

66

News reaches you that a group of Jewish workers led by **Arkady Kremer** have founded the **Jewish Workingmen's Party of Russia, Poland, and Lithuania**. (It's usually simply called "The **Bund**"—a lot easier to say!)

The **Bund** stresses the worth of Jewish workers. It has little use for those Jews who pretend not to be Jewish. "We have our dignity and our rights," Bundist leaders say. "We can be very Jewish and still stand for freedom and equality and better working conditions and higher pay. We may have to strike to get what we want, and we're willing to march on the picket lines, even to suffer, but we're determined. We won't give in!"

You believe in what the **Bund** stands for, and you join.

Turn to page 22.

67

The prophet wrote that the Messiah will ride into **Jerusalem** on a white donkey through the eastern gate, a teaching you have taken to heart. So, you find a small room that overlooks that area. You want to be one of the first to see this blessed figure.

You spend your days, even late into the night, studying the mystic literature of the **Kabbalah** and praying for the coming of that day when all of your troubles will be made right, when good people will be rewarded for their *mitzvot* and evildoers will receive their just punishments.

As you grow older, you continue waiting. True, the Messiah has not yet come, but he will. It is written in the holy books, so it must be so. You are content to live out your life here, prepared to greet this holy messenger of God.

END

68

You wish you could devote your entire life to helping the most needy and desperate of your people in the **Pale of Settlement**. But you are afraid. Will you, yourself, be caught up in the grinding poverty that devastates so many lives?

While you are thinking about what to do, you hear that oil has been found in the **Caspian Sea** near the city of **Baku** in **Azerbaijan**. The British Petroleum Company is beginning to develop this resource, and they are looking for good, intelligent workers.

You decide that you are not prepared to allow yourself to be destroyed by the **tzar**'s anti-Semitic laws and the mobs' pogroms. It is not permitted for a Jew to commit suicide, and to stay in the **Pale**, you think, would be killing yourself.

So, you move to **Baku**, go to work for British Petroleum, and spend the rest of your life earning a decent living, doing worthwhile work, and raising your family. You are sure that you have made a good choice.

END

69

The Jews of **Berditchev** are craftsmen and traders—towns-people. Without the farm products that Russian peasants grow, they would starve. They are a microcosm of the whole Jewish people—a nation, a religion, and a culture lacking a very important part. Until Jews learn to grow their own food and become self-sufficient, they will always be at the mercy of others.

"We must really become an Eternal People," you tell the others. "We shall teach ourselves agricultural skills." And so you and the others join a group called **Am Olam**. Under the banner of a plow and the Ten Commandments, your group of young men and women spend several years training as Jewish farmers.

But you can't succeed in **Russia**. The **May Laws** forbid you to own a farm. And to lease would throw you back into the control of Russians. You decide: we shall go elsewhere. Perhaps you will make *aliyah* and join one of the new **kibbutzim** in Palestine, or perhaps you will go to one of **Am Olam**'s colonies in America. You do not know, but you are sure that your future lies outside of **Russia**.

END

70

Y ou had not understood the evil of the tzarist government and how totally anti-Semitic it is. Now, the truth comes home to you in a way that you cannot escape, and you realize that there is only one solution: revolution. The **tzar** must go; his government must be overthrown.

You stay near the base and begin to teach the soldiers who come to the tavern. Slowly, you convince them that the workers of Russia will lead the revolution, but that the army must support them. "It is the only way," you tell them. "You can make a real difference if you are prepared to join the workers in their fight for freedom and a decent life."

When the revolution does break out on March 1, 1917, you and your troops are too far away to take part in the active fighting. But, together, you march into **Chelyabinsk** and stand with the working men and women of the city in solidarity. Some of them want to ally with the **Menshevik** party and some with the **Bolsheviks**. It doesn't matter to you; all that counts is that you are part of a glorious change in Russian life.

END

71

How can anyone accept this unfair, unethical, immoral system, you think to yourself. It violates everything you have been taught at home and in the synagogue since you were a little child. No! This is one compromise you will not make.

A **Communist** leader, **Vladimir Ilyich Lenin**, has been preaching the overthrow of the tzarist government. He is a wanted man; if he should be arrested, he would certainly be shot. So, he now lives in exile in **Vyborg, Finland**, just across the border of **Russia**. From that safer place, he sends letters and other writings, he receives visitors, and he continues to spread his revolutionary ideas.

You visit **Lenin** in his refuge and find him persuasive. With your experience in arranging for supplies for large groups of people, you will be useful to **Lenin** when the revolution breaks out—and he assures you it will. This is a cause to which you can commit your life… and you gladly do. Anything will be better for **Russia** and for the Jews than life under the **tzar**.

END

72

You flee **Russia**, across **Poland** and **Germany**, all the way to **Geneva**, a center of activity for Russian revolutionaries who, like yourself, have had to go into exile. There, you find **Vladimir Medem**, born a Jew, but baptized a Russian Orthodox Christian by his parents when he was an infant, and now a **socialist**.

Medem still has great feelings of warmth for Judaism, in spite of his conversion. He has allied himself with the **Bund**, the **Jewish Workingmen's Party of Russia, Poland, and Lithuania**. From **Geneva**, he advises **Bund** members on how to strive for workers' rights and how to better their conditions. **Medem** does what you would like to do, so you join his effort.

Unfortunately, so do the **Okhrana**, the Russian police. They plant a secret agent in **Medem**'s group. His job is simple: assassinate this troublemaker as soon as possible.

Late one evening, as you and **Medem** walk home along the Rue du Rhone, a man steps from the shadows and pulls a pistol from his coat. He fires, but his aim is bad. The last thing you feel is a searing pain in your chest. As you fall to the ground, you think, "At least I shall die for a good cause." And you do.

END

73

Y ou are depressed! You are disappointed! You are sad! How tragic that none of the rabbis you speak to seem to care about the welfare of Jewish workers—or even think that the Jewish religion has much to say about how the men and women who slave in factories are treated. This kind of Judaism is not for you. Who can think about the minute rules of *kashrut* when Jews cannot afford to feed themselves?

A young student who has been in **Berlin** tells you that there is another kind of Judaism. What a surprise! You have always been taught that there is Judaism… and there is Judaism. Some Jews may be **Chasidim** and some may be **Mitnagdim**, but they are really all the same. Now, you learn there is something different.

You take the train to **Berlin** and enroll at **Die Hochschule für die Wissenschaft des Judentums**, the school for the scientific study of Judaism and the rabbinical academy of liberal Judaism. A young rabbi, **Leo Baeck**, lectures on modern ethical problems and Judaism. Clearly, you have found the right place. Liberal Judaism is where you will spend the rest of your life.

END

74

Alexander III is no friend of the Jewish people. "**Russia**," he says, "should belong to the Russian people." He certainly does not think of Jews as Russians, and his actions bear this out. In 1891, the Jewish residents of **Moscow** are expelled and forced into the **Pale of Settlement**. More anti-Jewish laws are passed; life is getting even more difficult for Jews.

Even if **Pinsker** is right, even if Jews become "normal" like other people, there will be no place for Jews in **Russia**. The **tzar** and his ministers have made that very clear.

You might like to go to **Palestine**, but getting there is not easy. And everywhere there are advertisements for travel to **America**. Steamship companies have even set up offices where you can get advice and buy your tickets in advance.

That is what you do. You will go to **New York City**. Your dreams will come true, and you will work with labor unions to help other Jews achieve their goals. That will surely be a satisfying life.

END

75

Everyone tells you that **Isaac Leib Peretz** is the man you must see. "He knows everyone... the German philosophers Schopenhauer and Nietzsche... the Russian writer Gorky... everyone. And yet he still has touch with the common people. He can help you achieve your goal."

And **Peretz** does. This literary master finds you a place writing for a **Yiddish** newspaper where you can continue to share your **socialist** principles with *amcha*, with average, every-day Jews. It's a rewarding life, exciting, stimulating. You hope it goes on forever.

But it doesn't. In 1915, the government bans your paper. The war with **Germany** gives them emergency powers, and they use them to stifle any opposition. You are forced into exile once again, this time to **New York City**. There, you continue your **Yiddish** journalism as a writer for the *Forwarts*, and you spend the rest of your days on **East Broadway** in the **Lower East Side**, sharing your idea of a better world with anyone who will read your articles.

END

76

You return to **Russia** with **Axelrod** and join the **Menshevik** party. It seems to offer the best chance of success. Even though they are the minority group within the **Social Democratic Workers' Party**, they have made alliances with other groups, and that, you think, will help them govern democratically when the revolution comes.

But that's not what happens. In 1917, after the **Russian Social Democratic Labor Party** takes power, it is the **Bolshevik** group that is in control. Their leader, **V. I. Lenin**, demands strict discipline and agreement with what he believes. No dissent within the party is allowed.

You realize that you have made the wrong choice, and you switch your allegiance. Being a **Menshevik** or a **Bolshevik** is not so important; what counts is that the revolution succeeds. It does, but not before you are arrested as a potentially disloyal former **Menshevik**. The last thing you remember as you stand before the firing squad is that you did make a difference. Perhaps the sacrifice of your life for the revolution is not too high a price.

END

77

Life for you is hardly easy. Every day, you—and most other Jews—work long hours just to afford the barest necessities of life. You scrape together enough money at the end of the day to buy a loaf of coarse bread and a little *schmaltz* to spread on it. From the garden behind your hut, you have some carrots, onions, and potatoes. Meat? Hardly! Maybe you can manage a skinny chicken once a month or so, but that's a real luxury. And even your **Shabbos** clothing is so threadbare that you'd be embarrassed to go to *shul* if it wasn't that virtually every Jew is in the same situation.

The way things are, the *status quo*, isn't working for Jews. There must be a change. The only question is how to make a difference for the better. What you know for sure is that almost anything would be an improvement compared to how life is now.

Turn to page 27.

78

Y ou journey to the city of **Ekaterinoslav** on the **Dnieper River** in the **Ukraine**. A group of young Jewish workers have formed a new organization there; they have put forth a plan that very much interests you.

What they propose to do is to sponsor worker-run cooperatives in **Palestine**. These associations will be run on **socialist** principles, and when someone from the Russian group is ready to go on *aliyah*, that individual will have a ready-made place to settle, a job, and a home. It sounds to you that they are putting their ideas into practice, and you are so impressed that you join them. They call themselves **Po'alei Tzion**, "The Workers of Zion."

Soon you sense you are prepared for the big step of *aliyah*, but you are pretty sure you're not a good candidate for a **kibbutz**. Instead, you take the train to **Odessa** and then a boat to **Jaffa**. There is no Jewish town in this area, but a group of Jews have bought some land. They call it **Ahuzat Bayit**, and they intend to build a modern city there. Meanwhile, they live in tents. You join their group. Life may be tough right now, but you are sure that there is a bright future in front of all of you.

END

79

The city of **Kiev** lies only 350 miles north of **Odessa**, but as far as you are concerned, it is in a different, medieval world. Anti-Semitic propaganda and acts are common in **Kiev**, so it should not have been such a surprise to learn that the most horrible accusation against a Jew surfaced here.

March 1911: the police arrest **Mendel Beilis**. The charge: he has killed a Christian child before **Pesach**, draining its blood to mix with the matzah of the holy day. Most people believe that the police know who the real killer is but that they have a hidden motive for targeting a Jew. (Maybe they want to scare anyone who is pushing for democratic changes.) **Beilis** is certainly not guilty, but the police are withholding evidence and not telling what they really know.

Even in **Kiev**, this attack on Jews is outrageous. It's evil. It takes weeks before you can believe that it is really taking place. Then, you decide you must take action.

Turn to page 26.

80

If young Jews can learn what **Dubnow** is expressing, they will become leaders of this special people. You commit yourself to a career as their teacher. It is a noble, fine choice.

But the Russian government doesn't quite agree. Year by year, they restrict the number of your people's sons and daughters who are allowed to attend schools. Oh, yes, they can go to their own *cheders* and *yeshivot*. But sit in class with young Russian students? That will not be tolerated.

Without education, people remain slaves, and you understand that this is exactly what the government wants—Jews to be kept in a status of permanent slavery. No rights, no privileges, no spiritual nationhood. Just hard, filthy work and barely enough money to survive. That's all they think you deserve, and that's all they'll permit you to have. Closing the schools to your young people ensures that result.

Turn to page 40.

81

The sound of weeping and lament pierces you as though it were **Tishah Be'av**. You wade through the sewers of **Belz**, collecting torn sheets of the sacred Torah and other holy books. Then, you join the community at the cemetery, where you bury these fragments of your most precious possessions with the greatest honor.

When you return from the cemetery, you decide that you will never again suffer such a painful moment. "We may not be able to prevent an attack, but we shall be ready to resist it. Of that, one can be sure!"

You travel to **Odessa** where **Vladimir Jabotinsky** has organized a Jewish defense group. These young **Zionists** have acquired weapons and leave the city every *Shabbos* to engage in training. "Never again!" is their pledge.

When World War I breaks out, **Jabotinsky** offers his troops to the British army, and you become the core of the Jewish Legion, the first Jewish army unit in over 1,800 years. As you march down the street in your uniform, carrying your rifle, you are proud. "We are a new breed of Jews. We shall never again let anyone destroy our future."

END

82

An uprising has occurred. While you were thinking about what to do next, others took action. In October 1905, the masses revolted against the **tzar**'s absolute rule and, to everyone's surprise, forced the monarch to create a **Duma**, a Russian parliament.

But just as you rejoice at this beginning of popular representation, the **Narodnaya Volya** make a statement. "There is no place in **Russia**," these ultranationalist anti-Semites hold, "for Jews. Even Jewish workers are aliens, foreigners who can never belong to the true Russian people."

Appeals to **Nicholas II** are in vain. The **tzar** supports the intolerance of those who would exclude Jews from any role in the Russian future.

*If you despair of any Jewish future in **Russia** and look for a new life elsewhere,*
turn to page 126.

*If you cannot believe that Jews will be expelled from a democratic **Russia**,*
turn to page 15.

83

A meeting, called the **National Conference of Russian Jews**, is held in **Vilna**. All of the most important Jewish leaders of **Russia**, with the exception of the **Bund**, are present, and they debate for many days how to change the conditions of Jewish life for the better. The conference ends with the adoption of a program of demands to be presented to the government. It speaks of political and national rights for Jews and strives to gain equality of treatment for Jewish people.

When the petition is presented to the **tzar**'s chief minister, he laughs and tears it into several pieces. "What makes you think that his imperial majesty would even consider such ideas? I would not insult the **tzar** by asking him to read your pitiful words." The conference is powerless to move forward; its efforts are dead.

In your frustration, you turn to another path, a road of stronger action in concert with radicals from other groups.

Turn to page 123.

84

You attend the founding meeting of the **National Conference of Russian Jews** and listen to long speeches. Every group, other than the **Bund**, has sent delegates; it is the first widely-representative assembly of all Russian Jewry.

What you hear and read makes you furious. The Russians have made all **Zionist** activity illegal. Unfortunately, all the rumors are confirmed. You must proceed very cautiously and quietly.

Unless… unless… unless you decide that there is no hope for a **Zionist** movement in **Russia** and that you must act on your beliefs. You must pack up everything you own and move at once to **Jerusalem**. That will surely show the Russian government that they cannot stifle the urge of Jews to have a place they can call their own.

Defiantly, you take action. By train, by ship, and finally, by camel, you traverse the distance that separates you from the only part of the **Second Holy Temple** that still remains, the **Western Wall**. The very first thing you do when you arrive at this most sacred spot is to write a prayer on a little piece of paper. You stuff your *kvitel* between two rocks and recite the ancient words, "Next year may all Jews gather in **Jerusalem**." And you thank God that it has been your blessed fate to fulfill this dream.

Turn to page 67.

85

The **Uganda Plan** is one way to save Jewish lives, but certainly not the only one. Besides, you don't think it will become a reality. Many Jewish leaders are opposed, and the nations of the world are reluctant to support it.

You remind yourself that the chief goal is to relieve suffering and to ease the terrible conditions under which most of the Jews of **Russia** live their lives. On this point, Jews from all over the world are in agreement.

A group of Jews from across the **Atlantic Ocean** have created a new organization, the **American Jewish Joint Distribution Committee** (the "Joint"). These wealthy leaders share your ideals, and now they are raising money to send food, clothing, and other kinds of assistance to the impoverished and oppressed Jews of **Russia**. You go to work for the Joint and spend the rest of your life as the agent who distributes their *tzedakah* where it is needed the most. This is a wonderful career for you. You are acting on the highest Jewish values and making a real difference.

END

86

As the German army marches eastward toward **Russia**, you forget the pogroms and the attacks you have suffered. All you can think about is defending your homeland.

You join the Russian army and are sent quickly to the front lines. But it's not as you imagined. All around you is death and disease, mud and hunger, and not just among the soldiers. Civilians, women and children, even old people are caught up in the fighting. They suffer terribly, and Jews more than most, as the combat surges first in one direction, then the other through the **Pale of Settlement**.

As if that weren't bad enough, the non-Jews in your military unit never let you forget that you are a hated Jew. *Zhid*, they swear at you, even though you are risking your life to protect Mother Russia.

It's clear. There is no future for you in **Russia**. There is only one choice. As soon as possible you leave the country. Sad as it may be, you must make your life in another land.

END

87

Texas! **Texas?** What is a nice Jewish person like you from a *shtetl* in **Russia** doing in **Galveston, Texas**? It's an adventure. Cowboys! You've never seen a Reform rabbi, but **Rabbi Henry Cohen** meets every boat. He finds any Jewish passengers and makes sure they get settled.

You open the **Jewish Colonization Association** (ICA) office near the port and join **Rabbi Cohen** as each new ship arrives. You help the Jewish refugees through the immigration process, then see that they have a meal that is as close to kosher as possible, and make sure that they have somewhere to sleep.

Tomorrow, you will help them move along the trail to the towns and cities where others will give them more permanent homes and jobs and teach them what it means to live in America. At least these Jews have escaped the pogroms of the **Cossacks**, and at least they are not living in the tenements of **the Lower East Side** of **New York City**.

Your work ends when American immigration authorities make coming into **Galveston** impossible for Jews. But you will always look back warmly on this phase of your life. You have done sacred work, and you are very proud of what you have accomplished.

END

88

You travel as quickly as possible to the town of **Balta** in **Podolia**. There, you speak with the leaders of the Jewish community. They don't believe you, but the young workers and merchants do. They arm themselves as best they can. Some find a few rifles and pistols; most have wooden clubs and pointed pitchforks. Now, you wait.

When the rioters arrive, strutting into the main square, the Jewish self-defense forces attack them. The mob is stunned; they thought that they would face fearful, trembling, hiding Jews. This is very different. Bloodied, they retreat.

But not for long. Soon, a detachment of horse soldiers arrives, and the pogromniks regain their enthusiasm. While the troops protect them, they race through the Jewish section of **Balta**, destroying stores and houses, killing and injuring as many Jews as they can catch.

You emerge from hiding when the mob leaves and realize that self-defense can only be a temporary solution. It only delays the ultimate fate of **Russia**'s Jews.

Turn to page 26.

89

As the minister's words and **Gunzberg**'s interpretation of them sink in, you feel ill. For such a long time, you have believed—really believed—that Russians would accept Jews if they only understood more about them.

Now, it's obviously not possible to trust such thoughts any longer.

If such a well-informed and rational person as the minister thinks this way, anti-Semitism must be even worse among the common folk.

Your most cherished hopes are crushed. All that you believed is illusion. You had committed yourself to ideas that have now proved to be totally false.

Your future can only lie in one direction.
Turn to page 109.

90

The **Trans-Siberian Railway** runs just outside **Chelyabinsk**, the city where the military base is located. If you can find a way to get these Jewish soldiers on the train, they can travel through **Omsk** to **Irkutsk**, then across northern **Manchuria**, and finally to the port of **Vladivostok**. From there, they can certainly find a ship to **Japan** and freedom. The real question is, how to get them on the train in the first place?

You and the commander of the base are drinking vodka one evening when you come up with a plan. "These Jewish soldiers," you lean over and confide in him, "haven't seen a synagogue in a long time. If they could see how old and unpleasant it is, they would surely convert to Russian Orthodox Christianity. Let me take them to services on Yom Kippur. You'll see that I'm right."

A little drunk—which you counted on—he agrees. A few weeks later, on this holiest of all Jewish days, you lead a parade of Jews toward the synagogue. Except, of course, you all board the train. You bribe the conductor to let all of you stay on board, and ten days later, you are in **Vladivostok**. Freedom is only a few miles of sea away. You have saved some Jewish lives.

END

91

Y ou've tried every other approach: political negotiation, strikes, self-defense ... all sorts of tactics to protect Jews. And every time you found a new idea, **Nicholas II** and the anti-Semitic parties who support him rejected it and mounted new attacks on Jews... more pogroms... more anti-Jewish regulations and restrictions. And less freedom and less hope.

No, there is no other way. You join a secret society of **anarchists**. **Russia** has become so evil that it must be destroyed, by violence if necessary. Across the countryside, small bands ambush government officials and assassinate them; several thousand are killed. You realize that what you are doing violates one of the Ten Commandments, but you see no other path toward change.

It may not be right, but **anarchism** is your only hope... your last hope ... and you will die trying to make **Russia** a better country.

END

92

Hardly have you begun to walk on the protest line than the police appear. They arrest you and march all of you off to a foul-smelling, crowded jail. Only the fact that you know **Maxim Vinaver** saves you from being sent to a work camp in **Siberia**—where, you know, most of the prisoners die from starvation and overwork.

Vinaver scolds you. "That was a stupid move. Yes, of course, there need to be changes, but they can only come slowly, gradually. If you try to get too much too quickly, the **tzar** and his forces will crack down on you, and then what will you have? Nothing, but a slow and painful death in an awful prison camp."

What **Vinaver** says makes sense. You are sorry that you were so reckless. It's a good lesson that you learned. Now, you resolve to move forward, but more cautiously.

Turn to page 83.

93

You go to work as a writer for a newspaper in **St. Petersburg,** *Di Arbeiter Stimme*, "The Voice of the Worker." It's published in **Yiddish** so that average working people can read it easily and understand it. In its pages are articles about secret **socialist** societies, calls for action, but also lessons in reading, writing, and arithmetic for Jews who have not been able to go to school.

The first of May each year is a special day for workers. On that day, as the winter ice melts in this northern city, crowds of working men and women fill the streets, marching with banners: "Workers Unite!" "Down With the Oppressors!" Naturally, you join the marches.

Alexander III chose to ignore these protests, but **Nicholas II**, his son, calls out cavalry soldiers with sabers and foot soldiers with clubs. Before you have a chance to retreat, they rush down upon you. Blood is spilled, bones are broken, and many people are hauled off to jail.

You cannot believe that Russians would attack you—you, the workers who have made this country what it is. But they did, and now you have lost all hope for peaceful change.

Turn to page 71.

94

What excitement! What exhilaration! Sunday, January 9, 1905. Over 200,000 people stand in front of the **Winter Palace**. Some of them raise religious icons high above their heads. Leaders of the group present petitions to representatives of the government, asking for the establishment of a democratic assembly. This is the largest protest march ever held in **Russia**, and you are glad to be part of it.

Suddenly, you hear the crackle of gunshots. Around you, men and women fall to the street, some screaming, others lying still. You slip on their spilled blood as you scramble to get away. But you don't make it. Two burly policemen grab you and throw you to the ground, beat you without mercy, and then haul you away to prison.

This day will always be known as "Bloody Sunday." You think you will remember it for a very long time, but that is not to be. A few days later, you are dragged into the courtyard of the prison, tied to a post, and executed by a firing squad. The impact of this terrible day will live forever, but your life is over.

END

95

Chibbat **Tzion** is a group of young Jews who have adopted **Pinsker**'s theory. On *Shabbos*, instead of going to the synagogue, you travel outside **St. Petersburg** and learn how to farm the land. One day, you will work like a normal person, raising crops in your own land.

The government takes a dim view of your activities. "Your constant complaining, your talk of 'normalization,' your preparing to leave—all of these actions are insults to **Russia**. They make it seem as though we persecute you. Stop what you are doing...or else!"

If even these mild activities must be stopped, you understand that you can have no future in **Russia**. But you have heard of a country, a country with vast tracts of land that await willing farmers, a land that will welcome you with open arms and without anti-Semitism. It's awfully far away, on the other side of the globe, but that's where you will settle. Later, you can move to **Palestine**.

And so you travel by ship for weeks and weeks until you finally enter a beautiful harbor. **Australia** is a paradise, and you will live there happily, as a free Jew, as a free person for the rest of your life.

END

96

You return to the *shtetl* where you were born, but everything is now different. Many of the people you once knew are gone, forced to move into the **Pale of Settlement**. None of your family still resides in this town. You feel disconnected and apart.

The long years in prison have robbed you of your Jewish loyalties, too. The synagogue with its strange rituals, alien Hebrew language, and outdated ideas is not a comfortable place for you. You've been away from your people for so long that you cannot restore the links that once made being a Jew central to your existence.

Alone... friendless... without any community... disillusioned... isolated... very, very sad... you spend the rest of your days in a cold and solitary room. When you die, no one mourns. Your life has been a forfeit to the revolution, and you will never know whether it will succeed in the future or not. All you can do is hope so.

END

97

For nearly 2,000 years, Jews have wandered from place to place, never really being at home, never settled, never permanent. So, you are no different from your ancestors, living your life in *galut*, in exile in one place or another.

You write; you teach; you send letters, corresponding with radical groups in **Russia**. But the more you stay away from home—even though home is **Russia** and not very hospitable to Jews—the more you understand that you are still a Jew, a child of your father and your grandfather and many generations before them. Your life is wandering, seeking to make real the dreams of the prophets whose words you had studied in *Cheder* so many years ago.

As you come to the end of your life, you realize that you can be a citizen of the world, that you can stop being a Jew intellectually. But you can never sever the emotional connections you have with your people. No matter how you try, you will always be a Jew.

END

98

P. **Krushevan**, the editor-in-chief of the anti-Semitic newspaper *Bessarabets*, had used the pages of that journal to incite the mob. You know that this was a clever way of diverting attention from the real causes of Russian misery: corruption, inefficiency, economic mismanagement, and failure. But the diversion worked, and the mob took out its frustrations on the Jews.

Now, it's time to pay him back. With **Pinchas Dashevsky**, you acquire a pistol. You will come up to **Krushevan** on the street and stop him to ask a question. Then, **Dashevsky** will dash up and put a bullet through his brain.

But the plan fails because the pistol misfires. The two of you are arrested and hanged. You had wanted revenge, but the only consequence of your action is that the pogroms continue. Jews suffered, anti-Semites crowed their victory, and you are dead.

END

99

What's happening to Jews is also happening to others—peasants, workers, to many groups. If the **tzar** can oppress Jews, he can do the same to anyone. And, you believe, every Russian who loves freedom must speak out against all tyranny.

Of all the intellectuals and writers that **Russia** has produced, Ivan Turgenev and his younger colleague, Count Leo Tolstoy, ought to appreciate this situation. Both have written about freedom, the former in his novel about the conflict between two generations, *Fathers and Sons*, and the latter in his long book, *War and Peace*, about Napoleon's invasion of **Russia**. Surely, they must be concerned.

But they are not. "Jews? They are not our business. Let them find another country; they don't belong in **Russia**."

You are devastated. Russians who ought to speak out instead deliberately keep silent.

If you set out on a course to change non-Jewish attitudes,
turn to page 125.

*If you seek out a non-Jewish journalist outside **Russia**,*
turn to page 129.

100

As a member of **Bnai Moshe**, you discover a purpose for your life: creating a strong Jewish homeland in **Palestine**. But most of the Jews you meet in **Odessa** have been so affected by modern life and by the *Haskalah*, by the Jewish response to modern life, that they have lost their direction. Confused, they cannot make judgments about what is right and what is wrong, what is acceptable behavior and what is not. Those choices used to be made according to the *halachah*; these modern Jews have rejected that old religious law, but they have found nothing to replace it. Of course, that's why **Ahad Ha-Am** has developed his new teaching.

Many of his followers are working with governments, especially the British, to establish a Jewish state in **Palestine**. If they succeed, they will need schools and hospitals, roads, sewers, concert halls… all the institutions that make up a society. You begin to work for the **Jewish Colonial Trust**, the fund-raising body that will pay for all these improvements. And that choice proves to be so satisfying that you spend the rest of your life doing this important work.

END

101

One young man impresses you more than all the others. His wounds are not too serious, but his attitude is. He reads all the time.

At first, you assume that the books on his table are in **Yiddish**. As you talk with him, however, you discover that he is a disciple of **Eliezer ben Yehuda** and that his passion is to create a modern form of the ancient Hebrew language.

Eventually, the two of you fall in love and marry. Both of you teach, he in a school run by the **Bnai Moshe** and you at **Beis Ya'akov**. Jews, both of you believe, must have their own language, a language they can speak and write, a language that will make them like the other nations of the world, a language that will bring them respect and honor and that will connect them to the ancient civilization of the Bible.

In **Russia** and later in **Palestine**, both of you spend the rest of your lives learning and teaching Hebrew. The ancient language comes alive, as you find new words for modern ideas and objects. As a couple, you publish a Hebrew-language newspaper; your son is the first child in the world to be raised speaking modern Hebrew. What a wonderful purpose you have found! You are completely at peace.

END

102

By the time you arrive in **Palestine**, **Gordon** has already created a small group of people who share his ideas. He calls them **Hapoel Hatzair**, "Young Workers." Most of them live on **kibbutzim**, but even those who live in towns come out to the country for long periods and work side by side with *chalutzim*.

Together, you are building a new home for Jews, a land where Jews do not shun normal jobs. You gain a sense of power, knowing that in this new society Jews work the fields, like peasants in every country; Jews clean city streets and raise animals and build houses and work in hospitals and do every other jobs that all other people do. "We are no longer a different people," you think. "And now that we are like everyone else, there will no longer be a reason to hate us."

Your optimism may or may not be realistic, but your life is pure and wholesome. Your muscles grow and you feel a sense of control over your existence that Jews have not felt since they were exiled from **Jerusalem** by the Romans over 1,800 years ago. To feel such purpose gives you a wonderful sense of power, and you live out your life in the belief that you are really making a difference.

END

103

About 350 kilometers east of **Vilna** lies a little town named **Vitebsk**. There isn't much happening in this *shtetl*, except for the work of its most famous resident, a painter named **Marc Segal**. He has come back from **Paris** and **Berlin**, where his work was well-received. His French friend, Pablo Picasso, told him that his real name was too Jewish and that he ought to change it. So now he goes by a French-sounding version, **Chagall**, and people seem even more eager to buy his fantastic paintings.

The brilliant blue and vivid yellow colors of his art draw you in, and you stand in front of some of the pictures for a long time. People float through the air, fiddlers stand on the rooftops, animals take on nearly human forms, colors are often different than they would be in real life—this is really exciting art.

Chagall takes you on as an apprentice, a helper who will clean his brushes and touch up the paintings. You are learning, and you are sure that this is a career that will give you a great deal of joy through many years of artistic creation.

END

104

As far as you can see, there is really only one hope: to convince some government to sponsor the idea that the area of **Palestine** will be the Jewish home. **Great Britain** is the most likely choice, although you'll accept help from anywhere.

Together with **Herzl** and a brilliant chemist, **Chaim Weizmann**, you criss-cross Europe, meeting with the leaders of every country who will listen to you.

Only one, **Lord Arthur James Balfour**, a British states-man, seems sympathetic, and then only because he wants **Weizmann** to help the British navy with the more powerful gunpowder he has developed. If that's the price for saving Jewish lives from Russian pogroms, so be it.

You spend the rest of your life working with these **Zionist** leaders to make **Herzl**'s dream come true. Nothing you could do with your life would have more meaning than to re-create a Jewish state where Jews could come, live in safety, and develop their own culture and civilization. That is your destiny, and you will pursue it.

END

105

You meet with other **Zionist** leaders at a Russian Zionist Congress. Certainly, they can see that the highest priority must be to accept a plan that will save Jewish lives. Holding out for a homeland in **Palestine** will cost thousands, perhaps tens of thousands, of Jews their safety. *Piku'ach nefesh* is the most important value, you remind the assembly.

"Yes, of course. We know that. You don't have to tell us what is obvious. But it's also true that we have waited nearly two thousand years to return to the holiest city in the world, to **Jerusalem**. What's a few more years? And what's a few more Jewish lives, when Jews have died for their faith throughout the ages? We must reject the **Uganda Plan** and wait until we can create our own nation in **Palestine**."

You disagree, but your position is defeated. Most of the leaders agree that it will be **Palestine** or nothing. You leave the meeting, equally convinced that protesting the decisions of the **Zionist** leaders will do no good, nor will it help to speak out against the oppression sponsored by the Russian government.

Turn to page 115.

106

The **Chabad** school of **Chasidim** stresses thinking, studying, and serving God with joy and gladness. You are sure that you have made the right choice.

Dressed in your long black coat and **Shabbos** hat, you **daven** with other **Chasidim** in the **shul** that **Rabbi Menachem Mendel Schneerson** founded nearly a century ago. Your prayers rise up with special fervor as you chant loudly and sway vigorously. The **rebbe** reassures you: "**Moshiach** may not have come yet, but he will. There is no question."

The years pass, but the Messiah does not appear. Still, your faith is strong. "It is possible that we are too soon, that we must wait longer. But we cannot stop our efforts. If the Messiah does not come for me, then perhaps for my son, and if not then, maybe for my grandson. But **Moshiach** will surely come." Your faith is unshakable, and you feel your life has meaning as you strive to bring the Messiah to earth.

END

107

What a strange group of fellow voyagers you have found! The ship *Weser* sails with 820 **Orthodox** Jews from **Bratzlav**, **Berditchev** and **Medzibozh**, cities in the western Russian province of **Podolia**.

After four weeks at sea, the ship glides into the **Rio de la Plata** and pulls up to the docks of **Buenos Aires**. The new settlers will go on to the community of **Mauricio**, the first **Jewish Colonization Association** (ICA) settlement on the pampas, about 180 miles west of **Buenos Aires**.

You stay in the capital city to receive new boatloads of refugees. Their new lives are difficult. Most of them know nothing about farming and raising cattle; they have to be taught almost everything about their new existence.

You help them in every way you can. As your life draws toward a close, you can visit eighteen Jewish agricultural colonies with nearly 35,000 settlers. To have helped rescue that many people and given them the chance to make new, free, Jewish lives gives you the greatest satisfaction you can imagine.

END

108

A new organization has been established to help the Jews of the **Pale of Settlement**. It is called **ORT**, which is an abbreviation for its real Russian title, "Society for Manual Work." Its goal is to teach useful trades to Jews who have been forced to move into the **Pale** because of the **May Laws**. When the men can work, they can support their families. When they can support their families, many social problems will be eased.

For years, you *davened* **Maimonides' eight steps of** *tzedakah* at the end of the *Shabbos* morning *Musaf* service. Now, finally, you understand. The highest degree of charity is to teach a person a trade and to find him a job. Then he will never again need charity.

You find a position with **ORT**. It gives you great satisfaction to carry out this high Jewish value. You are living up to the best traditions of your people, doing a great *mitzvah*, and this makes your life feel very worthwhile.

END

109

As much as you understand that Russians hate Jews, you love **Russia**. It's strange that the language and the culture, the traditions, the scenery, and even the harsh winter are intensely special to you. If you were to leave, you would miss them terribly, perhaps more than you could bear.

But you also cannot accept the ongoing pain of being Jewish. You have suffered enough, and you certainly will not place this heavy burden on your children. Your decision is clear.

One afternoon, you stand on the **Nevsky Prospekt** and look across the **Yekaterinensky Canal**. There, you see the **Kazan Cathedral**. As if driven more by fate than by the words of **Pobedonostsev**, you walk across the street and into the church. There, you find a priest and explain to him that you must become a Russian Orthodox Christian.

He helps you convert. This is the end of your Jewish life. But it is also the beginning of an entire new life for you and your family. You hope you will be satisfied with your choice.

END

110

Surely, the minister must make statements like these for political purposes. But he can't really believe what he is saying. To ruin the economic opportunity of the Jews is to place the entire financial future of **Russia** at risk. He certainly would never do that.

That *Shabbos* falls during **Pesach**, and you go to services at the great **Choral Synagogue** on **Lermontovsky Prospekt**. For thousands of years, Jews have found comfort and wisdom through prayer; you hope to find answers to what you must do in the same way that your ancestors did.

The *Chazan* chants the *haftarah*, and you recognize the thirty-seventh chapter of Ezekiel... dry bones... coming back together... coming back to life. Now, you know what to do. There will be a future life for Jews in **Russia**. All you have to do is be patient, and things will work out all right. Just stay the course that you have planned out, and tomorrow will be better.

You leave the synagogue satisfied that you know how to proceed. You are sure you are right, and you are at peace.

END

111

Alerted and aroused, the Jews of **Berditchev** fight off the pogrom. But all of you understand that this victory is temporary. There are more Russians, more police, more soldiers with better weapons than you. Ultimately, if they want to attack in force—and you are sure they will—you will suffer.

The only real victory is to change Russian society so that no one wants to murder Jews, so that people do not need a scapegoat or a victim. Then, perhaps, all people can live in friendship.

On the street, in coffeehouses, in secret newspapers, you learn of a new group that is committed to just such a goal. They are called **Communists**, and they follow the idealistic teachings of **Karl Marx**. Each person will have what he or she needs; each person will contribute to society what he or she can. All people will be treated equally.

The promise of Communism attracts you. Certainly, tzarism hasn't been good for the Jews; this cannot be worse and may be a lot better. You leave **Berditchev**, determined to find a new home and a renewed purpose under **Marxism**.

Turn to page 123.

112

OK! That's the reality. You're just one individual, and the system is far bigger than you. If you want to make a living, you've got to accept what every other person does and join in. So, you do, and your military supply business thrives. In fact, you make a great deal of money.

On April 6, 1903—it was the last day of **Pesach**—the church bells begin to ring. A mob of non-Jews bursts into the street, as if by a prearranged sign, and attacks any Jew they can find. They dash into Jewish neighborhoods, destroying property, stealing whatever they discover, and beating defenseless Jews. "Rich and greedy" Jews become particular targets; the mob of looters assumes that they have gotten their wealth by illegal, underhanded means—and that means you.

You are badly hurt by the beatings, and all your hard-earned profits disappear. Nothing is left. You have only one alternative: you must flee Mother **Russia** and resettle elsewhere. You are grateful that you are still alive—some are not—and you begin the difficult job of starting your life over again.

END

113

The end of the first **Duma** is clearly a setback, but **Nicholas II** promises to organize a second one. "That's OK," you think. "After all, **Russia** has had no experience with democracy. It makes sense that starting off would be difficult. We can still have hope."

But the second **Duma** is even less powerful than the first. The number of Jews elected to it has dwindled to four. The **Black Hundreds** and the **Narodniki** have grown in power, and they now go on the attack. Bigotry and hatred, open incitement to violence against Jews—these are their standard speeches. And the Jews of **Russia** are more defenseless than ever against their venom, which can now flow over the floor of the **Duma** without restraint.

You see only one path left, the path that leads out of **Russia**. And even though you had hoped, with **Vinaver**, that you would not need to leave your homeland, now there is no other choice.

Turn to page 64.

114

Tevunah was written by **Rabbi Israel Lipkin**, who is also known by the name **Salanter**, for the town of **Salaty**, where he lived. He realized that Judaism had to address the most critical issues of the day, or it would become stale and dated. The movement that he began is called the **Musar movement** because it applies age-old Jewish ethics to modern problems.

What a remarkable find you have made! It's the combination that you have been looking for: Judaism and modern life.

You try to seek out disciples of **Israel Salanter**, but there are none in **St. Petersburg** or **Moscow**. Almost in despair, you learn that his ideas have begun to spread widely. There are now rabbis at a *yeshivah* in **Kovno** who could teach you Musar. You know that you must follow this path.

Turn to page 13.

115

It seems senseless to you to continue the protests. The **tzar**'s forces are so overwhelmingly strong that you stand no chance of prevailing. The only way you see to live in a more equal, fair society is to leave.

Word reaches you that there are settlements in **Palestine** called **moshavot**. There, everyone is treated equally. Each person works as much as he or she is able, and each person receives food and lodging, clothing, education, and whatever else is necessary. Every resident owns his or her own home and property, but everyone cooperates. Together, they are building a new society.

The mother of all **moshavot** is **Petach Tikvah**, a citrus-growing settlement a few miles inland from the **Mediterranean** coast. You travel southward by railway, then by sea from **Odessa** to **Jaffa**, and then by mule to the settlement. The minute you set foot on its grounds, you know you have made the right choice. You feel free for the first time in your life: free to live without fear, free to laugh, free to love. **Petach Tikvah** will be home for the rest of your life.

END

116

The nearest large city is **Odessa**, so you travel there as quickly as possible. What you find surprises you. **Odessa** has an intellectual tradition, but a very liberal one. Almost any kind of idea is accepted. You hear the most outrageous opinions in the coffeehouses and even in the vestry rooms of synagogues. More than that, people seem liberated from the traditional moral and ethical behaviors that you had always taken for granted.

To tell the truth, you are offended by the behavior of these **Odessa** Jews. This is not the freedom that you had hoped for. Yes, Jews need freedom, but you had expected that this would bring a spiritual sense of peace. What you see, instead, is simply wrong.

The kind of wholeness you seek, you imagine, would more likely be found in a rural setting. When everyone depends on each other, people could not act as these city Jews do.

You consider making **aliyah** *to a* **kibbutz** *in* **Palestine**. *If that is your choice,*
turn to page 124.

If you would rather join a local organization to learn more about agriculture,
turn to page 128.

117

Maybe the government will listen to the voice of reason. **Theodor Herzl** calls upon the minister of the interior, **Count von Plehve**, and asks him to lift the restrictions on **Zionist** activity. He promises that the **Zionists** will abstain from anti-government, revolutionary activities. Getting more Jews to move to **Palestine, Herzl** argues, will help solve **Russia**'s "Jewish problem." There won't be as many Jews for **Russia** to worry about.

But **von Plehve** has no interest in this proposal. If anything, he makes the restrictions tighter, outlawing all **Zionist** activity. **Constantine Pobedonostsev** has advised the **tzar** that he can solve the "Jewish problem" this way: "Put one-third of the Jews in the army, chase another one-third out of the country, and kill the last one-third." Some solution! You prefer the middle option, and you and nearly 2,500,000 Jews begin the slow, dangerous, and difficult journey out of **Russia**. Like the **Wandering Jew** of old, you will live somewhere new, but you will always be proud to be a Jew.

END

118

"So, you want to go back to **Jerusalem** and build a Jewish state?" the rabbi asks. The way he says it, it sounds like a challenge, not a question; but you stay quiet. "Your dream is idolatry. Only the Messiah will rebuild the holy city and cause the *Shechinah* to dwell in it. To try to hasten the coming of the Messiah is a sin. I forbid you to do this."

You stumble out of his house and squint in the bright sunlight. When your eyes adjust to the new light, you can see more clearly, and you understand that the rabbi's thinking may, in fact, be true. At one time, you thought God was depending on us to take the first steps. You were prepared to become an active **Zionist**. But now you have decided to trust your *rebbe*. He will guide you in Torah-true spiritual paths.

Turn to page 106.

119

Dubnow teaches that "knowledge of its history by an oppressed group is a political weapon." You decide to use this weapon by working as an organizer of the **Bund**, a Jewish workers' union. If you can help improve the day-to-day life of the Jewish people, surely they will become the more spiritual people that **Dubnow** wants them to be.

With **Arkady Kremer**, you travel from one small Jewish town to the next, teaching Jewish men and women how to come together in groups, how to bargain more effectively with their employers, how to live a better life.

But outside the Jewish community, things are not going well. The Russian army and navy have lost a war with **Japan**, and an old-new game has begun: "Let's blame the Jews for our defeat." Frustration leads to anti-Semitism, and all your talk of a spiritual people is not much of a defense against mobs of **Cossack** peasants.

Turn to page 34.

120

Some **Chasidic** men burst into the room. They elbow you away from the young man you are treating. "It's against God's will for a woman to have such contact with a man, especially a man who is not modestly clothed. We forbid you to continue this *hillul ha-Shem*."

You are shocked. Often, your own rabbi, as completely **Orthodox** as these men, has taught you that the *mitzvah* of *piku'ach nefesh*, of saving a life, is more important than anything else. That's what you are doing, and you know these intruders are wrong.

When they leave, pushed out of the hospital by some of the patients who have already regained a bit of strength, you try to sort out what has happened. It isn't wrong for you to touch a man, particularly if you are healing his wounds and restoring his spirit. That's a good thing to do. Someday, you decide, you will help build a hospital where **Orthodox** Judaism and medicine will work hand in hand to save Jewish lives. That ambition becomes the driving force in your life, and you spend the rest of your days pursuing this meaningful goal.

END

121

W ords of a poem resound from one dark corner of the *shul*. A young man is reciting from memory. "What are these verses?" you inquire.

"If you would know the mystic fountain from which your brethren ... drew strength and fortitude in evil days..." he repeats. Words of **Chayyim Nachman Bialik**, a brilliant young Russian Jew whose poetry has touched the soul of many. And what is this source of strength? You listen further and discover that **Bialik** is describing the synagogue and its books. If you want to be strong, go back, he says, to the very source of strength, to God and to the synagogue, where the study of the sacred books takes place.

Of course! He must be right! You devote the rest of your life to spreading this message among young Russian Jews who have forgotten the life-giving power of the tradition. If only they would become *ba'alei teshuvah*, if only they would return to the religion of their elders, all would be well. This is your mission: to preach the value of Judaism and the synagogue to the next generation. It is a cause to which you give yourself without reservation and with great energy. The future depends on your success.

END

122

A friend of yours introduces you to a middle-aged writer named **Solomon Rabinowitz**. "**Shalom Aleichem**," you say, and he responds, "That's right."

You explain to him that you want to become a writer, like he already is, wielding the **Yiddish** language as a weapon to convey both the humor and the tragedy of modern Jewish life. Can he help you tell the stories of the Jews of the **Pale of Settlement**?

"Why yes. I can do that. Of course, you'll have to find your own stories. I've already begun a tale about Tevye, the milkman, and his daughters. It's really not about Tevye, but about how the old ways of the father no longer work and how the new paths of the younger generation are difficult for everyone to live with."

You accept **Rabinowitz**'s offer of help and bid him farewell for the time being. "**Shalom Aleichem**," you wave to him, and he answers, "That's right." And you both smile broadly at your little joke.

END

123

The small man captures your attention with his huge words. **Leon Trotsky**, named **Davidovich Bronstein** at his *bris*, is one of the two men who leads the **Communist Party**. The other is **V. I. Lenin**, but he is in hiding right now, so **Trotsky** is the only spokesman you can hear. And it is an act of great courage for him to speak in public because the **Okhrana** are hot on his trail, always interested in arresting him.

Trotsky hates the **tzar**'s regime, its tyranny and injustices, its graft and exploitation and restrictions. Everything about the present government, he says, is evil, and it must be overthrown—with violence if necessary.

What he says makes sense to you, but there are two groups within the **Communist Party**, **Mensheviks**, and **Bolsheviks**. You cannot make up your mind with which to ally yourself. But something happens that solves your problem for you.

Turn to page 127.

124

At the southern end of the **Kinneret**, the Sea of Galilee, there is a new settlement, a **kibbutz** named **Deganiah**. On the **kibbutz**, no one owns any private property; everything is the possession of the **kibbutz**, and the residents simply are allowed to use whatever they require. It's at **Deganiah**, you understand, that **Karl Marx**'s idea, "To everyone according to his need," has really been put into practice.

Deganiah is where you go. You are sure that such a cooperative settlement demands that everyone behave in the most proper fashion; the survival of everyone depends, after all, on the actions of each member of the **kibbutz**. Your life will be difficult, but with everyone going in the same direction and pursuing the same goals, success is certain.

END

125

If the non-Jews only knew how rich and glorious the history and culture of the Jews of **Russia** is, they would change their attitudes. You believe that idea with all your heart.

And so you go to work with **S. An-Sky**, the head of the **Jewish Historical-Ethnographical Society**, to collect information about the history and achievements of Russian Jews. Even you are impressed; this is great material, and it will surely impress the leaders of Russian public opinion.

When another outbreak of pogroms occurs, you realize that anti-Semitism has nothing to do with facts and information. The people who want to hate Jews have already made up their minds; nothing will change them. You have chosen a particular way to make peace with your neighbors, and you have lost.

END

126

With all the possessions that matter to you, you begin walking west. A few pieces of clothing, an extra pair of shoes, a **siddur,** a *tallis*, two loaves of hard black bread... all of it in a bag slung over your shoulder. Things, however, mean less than the possibility that you could live in a free place where a Jew does not have to fear for his life every day.

It takes several months to walk from **Russia** to the port city of **Danzig** (**Gdansk** they call it in Polish). There, you find work shoveling coal on a tiny freighter that sails north around **Denmark**, across the **North Sea**, and into the port of **Rye, England**. You leave the ship and find your way to the **East End of London**.

In this bustling, noisy section of the city, Jews from Eastern Europe have created their own community. There are synagogues and markets, schools and restaurants. **Yiddish** is spoken more than English, and you are comforted to hear these familiar sounds. It feels good to walk these streets, and you are sure that you will be able to forge a solid and successful future for yourself in this place.

END

127

March 2, 1917. A date you will always remember. A date of historic importance. On that day, **Tzar Nicholas II** abdicates and turns the government of **Russia** over to a provisional government run by **Alexander Kerensky**. (**Trotsky** tells you privately that this government will not last and that the **Communists** will be in power before the snow falls. But on this wonderful day, who cares! All you want to do is celebrate the marvel of freedom.)

It dawns on you that today is just three days before **Pesach**, the Jewish festival of freedom. Over three thousand years ago, another pharaoh was forced to let your people go; now a modern oppressor has suffered the same fate. The Jews of **Russia** are emancipated; another liberation has occurred.

Whether the heady promises of the revolution will come true is for the future. Today, you take to the streets with many, many other cheering people. Today is a day for celebration.

END

128

The **Am Olam** chapter that you join in **Odessa** helps train you to be a forester, an expert in raising and caring for trees. Soon, a message is received that their colony in America needs people with your skills. You're young and daring, ready for an adventure, so you volunteer to go.

The colony is called **New Odessa**, and it is located in the state of **Oregon**, a place where there are, indeed, a lot of trees. Unfortunately, by the time you get there, the colony has folded. It just did not work.

You and the other pioneers move to the city of **Portland**, where you join **Beth Israel Congregation**. You are moved by the powerful sermons of its rabbi, **Stephen Samuel Wise**, and even after he leaves for **New York** and a new Reform pulpit, you continue to enjoy the ethical message that you hear nearly every *Shabbos* from the pulpit. This is where you belong, in a community with good standards of behavior and a real economic future. In **Portland**, you have found hope and a future.

END

129

Y ou don't have to look far; in a manner of speaking, he finds you!

The front page of the French newspaper, *L'Aurore*, of January 13, 1898, carries a headline story. Its first word, "**J'accuse**," (I accuse), becomes the battle cry of entire groups of Jews in **Russia**.

It turns out that the author, **Emile Zola**, discovered a scandal in the French army. After they lost a war against the Germans in 1871, they blamed the defeat on a Jewish artillery officer, **Captain Alfred Dreyfus**. Now, it turns out, **Dreyfus** was not the traitor; a **Major Esterhazy** probably was, but **Dreyfus** was convicted and sent to **Devil's Island** prison. **Zola** is demanding that he be brought back and given a new, fair trial.

You and many others are outraged that such an anti-Semitic act could have happened in **France**. In **Russia**, maybe, but in **France**? If it's possible there, then you must all do something very different.

Turn to page 25.

GLOSSARY

Ahad Ha-Am • See **Ginsberg, Asher**.

Achuzat Bayit • "Housing Property," a society founded in 1906 in Jaffa (**Palestine**) to acquire land for Jewish residence in an area just to the north. This area was later named Tel Aviv.

Alexander III • **Tzar** of Russia, 1881–1894; very anti-Semitic.

Aliyah • The departure from one's original home to settle in **Palestine**.

American Jewish Joint Distribution Committee • Organization created in 1914 to coordinate relief to Jewish victims of World War I. Continues in existence today.

Am Olam • Russian Jewish society (1881–1887) that founded agricultural colonies in the United States.

Anarchism, Anarchist • Idea or supporter of idea that each person should be free to make life choices with minimal interference from government; its supporters sometimes used violence to secure their goals.

An-Ski, S. • Alias of Solomon Zainwill Rapaport (1863–1920), a socialist writer.

Auto-Emancipation • Book written by **Leon Pinsker** in 1882, which called for the establishment of a Jewish national homeland.

Axelrod, Pavel • Revolutionary, founder of **Russian Social Democratic Party**. Lived in exile in Berlin and Geneva for many years.

Ba'alei teshuvah • "Repenters," Jews who had been nonobservant and became **Orthodox**.

Ba'al Shem Tov • See **Israel ben Eliezer**.

Baeck, Rabbi Leo (1874–1956) • Chief liberal rabbi of Germany until the onset of World War II, he was imprisoned in the*Theresienstadt* concentration camp but survived. He was a scholarly and compassionate leader of Jews.

Balfour, Lord Arthur James *(1848–1930)* • British statesman who signed the Balfour Declaration (November 2, 1917), declaring Britain's sympathy with **Zionist** goals.

Beilis, Mendel *(1874–1934)* • Victim of "blood libel" charges in Kiev; acquitted in 1913. He moved to the United States in 1920.

Beis Ya'akov • System of schools for **Orthodox** Jewish girls, which began in Cracow in 1917.

Beit hamidrash • Hebrew for "House of study," one of the ways to refer to a synagogue.

ben Yehuda, Eliezer *(1858–1922)* • Founder and developer of modern use of the Hebrew language.

Bessarabets • Anti-Semitic newspaper that encouraged attacks on Jews. Published by **P. Krushevan**.

Beth Israel Congregation • Reform Jewish temple in Portland, Oregon. Still exists as an active congregation.

Bialik, Chayyim Nachman (1873–1934) • Modern Hebrew author considered "the Hebrew national poet."

Black Hundreds • Armed, anti-Semitic groups who led pogroms; sponsored by the Union of the Russian People.

Bnai Moshe • "Sons of Moses," **Zionist** group founded in Odessa by **Ahad Ha-Am**.

Bnos Tzion • "Daughters of Zion," the Jewish Women's Federation of Poland.

Bolshevik • Majority group of Russian **socialists**, led by **Lenin**; eventually gained control over **Communist Party** and ruled the Union of Soviet Socialist Republics.

Bund • Jewish **socialist** workers' group founded in Vilna in 1897. Did not support Zionism.

Chabad • A branch of **Chasidism**, also called Lubavitch, founded by **Rabbi Shneur Zalman**. Stands for _chochmah_ (wisdom), _bina_ (understanding), and _da'at_ (knowledge).

Chagall, Marc (Marc Segal) (1887–1985) • Jewish painter who often used *shtetl* themes.

Chalutzim • "Pioneers," early settlers of **Palestine** (before 1948).

Chasid (Plural: Chasidim) • See page 12.

Chasidic • Related to Chasidism, a Jewish movement founded by the **Ba'al Shem Tov** (1699–1761).

Chasidism • Religious-social movement founded by **Israel ben Eliezer** about 1750, which stresses joy, prayer, and the hope that the Messiah will come.

Chazan • Cantor or prayer leader.

Cheder • Traditional Jewish elementary school.

Chibbat Tzion • A **Zionist** movement founded in 1882 that believed Jews should take specific actions, such as buying land in **Palestine** and preparing for aliyah; merged with the World Zionist Organization in 1919.

Cohen, Rabbi Henry (1863–1952) • American Reform Jewish rabbi in Galveston, Texas, who welcomed immigrants and helped them settle in the United States.

Communist Party, Communists • Russian political party and its members based on the ideas of **Karl Marx** and led by **Lenin**. Led the revolution against the **tzar** and became the new government.

Constitutional Democratic Party • See **Kadet**.

Cossacks • Elite cavalry units who had special loyalty to the **tzar**. Often used to put down peasant uprisings and urban strikes.

Daf gemora • "A page of Talmud"; scholarly **Orthodox** Jews often study one page every day.

Dashevsky, Pinchas (1879–1934) • **Zionist** activist who tried to assassinate **Krushevan**, the instigator of the pogroms in **Kishinev**.

Daven • To pray, often with a swaying motion and singsong voice.

Deganiah • A **kibbutz** established in 1909 on the shores of the Kinneret (Sea of Galilee); still functions today.

De Hirsch, Baron Maurice (1831–1896) • Philanthropist; founder of **Jewish Colonization Association** to help oppressed Jews find new and safer places to live.

Devil's Island • A terrible French prison on a Caribbean island.

Di Arbeiter Stimme • "The Voice of the Worker," **Yiddish** newspaper that expressed concerns of Jewish workers.

Die Hochshule für die Wissenschaft des Judentums (1872–1942) • "The Advanced School for the Scientific Study of Judaism," a scholarly institution and liberal rabbinical seminary in Berlin.

Dreyfus, Alfred (1859–1953) • French army officer convicted of treason in 1894, pardoned in 1899, and cleared in 1906. His trial motivated **Herzl** to create the **Zionist** movement.

Dubnow, Shimon (1860–1941) • Historian who taught the idea of Jewish national rights based on social and cultural independence, but not political separation.

Duma • The Russian parliament.

Esterhazy, Major Ferdinand Walsin (1847–1927) • A French army officer who was the true German spy, but who blamed **Alfred Dreyfus** and caused him to be treated as a traitor.

First Zionist Congress • Meeting organized by **Herzl** in 1897 in Basle (Switzerland) to coordinate and further efforts of **Zionists** from all countries.

Galut • The state of exile; living in the Diaspora.

Galveston, Texas • Port city where the **Jewish Colonization Association** brought tens of thousands of Eastern European Jewish immigrants so they would settle away from New York City.

Gemara • Together with the **Mishnah**, it makes up the **Talmud**.

Ginsberg, Asher (Ahad Ha-Am) (1856–1927) • Philosopher and **Zionist** leader.

Gittin • Section of the **Talmud** that deals with divorce.

Gordon, Aaron David (1856–1922) • Early **Zionist** who taught about the dignity of manual labor.

Gunzberg, Baron David (1857–1910) • Leader of **St. Petersburg** Jewry, scholar, and author.

Gunzberg, Baron Horace • Born near Kiev in 1833 and died in **St. Petersburg** in 1909, he was the chief spokesman for Russian Jews during the last twenty years of his life.

Habakkuk • A biblical prophet.

Halachah • Jewish law.

Hapoel Hatzair (1905–1922) • Labor **Zionist** movement in **Palestine**; Young Workers' Party.

Haskalah • Eighteenth-century movement of "Enlightenment" that put Jews in touch with modern learning and ideas.

Havdalah • "Separation," the service at the end of the Sabbath that divides it from the week that follows.

Herzl, Theodor (1860–1904) • Journalist; founded modern political Zionism in 1897 and worked tirelessly to establish a Jewish state.

Hillul ha-Shem • "Insult to God," any act that decreases respect for God.

Israel ben Eliezer (ca. 1700–1760) • Founder of **Chasidism**; also known as the **Ba'al Shem Tov**, "Master of the Good Name."

Jabotinsky, Vladimir (1880–1940) • **Zionist** who believed in taking vigorous, direct action; leader of the Jewish Legion during World War I; founder of the **Zionist** movement called Revisionism.

"J'accuse" • Editorial article by **Emile Zola** that reopened the **Dreyfus** case and led to public recognition of anti-Semitism in Europe.

Jewish Colonial Trust • Established by the World Zionist Congress in Vilna to purchase property in **Palestine** (1898).

Jewish Colonization Association (ICA) • Arm of the **Baron de Hirsch** Fund that helped settle Jews from Eastern Europe in Argentina, Texas, and elsewhere.

Jewish Historical-Ethnographical Society • Scholarly society of Jews in St. Petersburg that collected Jewish folklore, especially among **Chasidim** and in *shtetlach*. Headed by **S. An-Ski**.

Jewish Workingmen's Party of Russia, Poland, and Lithuania • The **Bund**.

Kabbalah • A Jewish mystical tradition.

Kadet • Constitutional Democratic Party founded by **Vinaver** in 1904 to represent the interests of Jews in the **Duma**.

Kashrut • The laws and practices relating to eating in a traditional way; keeping kosher.

Kerensky, Alexander (1881–1970) • Russian revolutionary and politician who led the provisional government between March and November 1917.

Kibbutz (Plural: kibbutzim) • Settlements in **Palestine** organized along **socialist** ideas where all property is owned in common.

Kishinev • City where vicious pogroms erupted in 1903.

Kittel • A white robe worn by men during the High Holy Days, Pesach, weddings, and by a corpse. It suggests purity.

Kremer, Arkady (1865–1935) • Founder and leader of the **Bund**.

Krushevan, P. • Leader of the anti-Semitic **Black Hundreds** and instigator of the **Kishinev** pogroms of 1903.

Kvitel • A small piece of paper containing a prayer or other message to God; usually inserted between the stones of the **Western Wall**.

L'Aurore • "The Dawn," a French newspaper, which published **Emile Zola**'s letter **"J'accuse."**

Lenin, Vladimir Ilyich (1870–1924) • Russian politician who led the Communist revolution that overthrew the **tzar** and created the Union of Soviet Socialist Republics.

Lipkin, Rabbi Israel (1810–1883) • Usually better known as **Israel Salanter**.

Lower East Side • Section of New York City where most Jewish immigrants settled when they first arrived in the United States.

Ma'ariv • The afternoon prayer service.

Maimonides' eight steps of *tzedakah* • In his *Mishneh Torah* (Gifts to the Poor X:7–14), Maimonides describes eight steps, from the most generous and anonymous charity to the least.

Martov • Leader of the Union of Russian People; he was very anti-Semitic.

Marx, Karl (1818–1883) • German philosopher, radical economist, and revolutionary leader whose "scientific socialism" became the basis for modern Communism.

Marxism • The philosophy of government based on the ideas of **Karl Marx**.

May Laws • Anti-Semitic laws enacted in 1882 under **Tzar Alexander III**.

Medem, Vladimir (1879–1923) • Leader of the **Bund**.

Menshevik, Menshevism • Minority party or philosophy of Russian **socialists** that lost out after 1917 to **Lenin** and the **Bolsheviks**.

Midrash • A type of nonlegal Jewish literature containing ethical and moral advice, anecdotes, fables, theology, philosophy, and biblical commentaries.

Mishnah • Legal commentary on the Bible compiled by the school of Judah the Prince about 200 C.E. in the Galilee.

Mitnagdim • Opponents of the **Chasidim**, centered in Lithuania.

Mishnaic • From *Mishnah*, the first written collection of the Oral Law. Its purpose was to explain the intention of the **Torah**, and it covered a broad scope of Jewish life.

Mitzvah (Plural: *Mitzvot*) • Hebrew word meaning "God's commandment." Usually used to mean a "good deed."

Mizrachi • **Orthodox Zionist** movement founded by **Isaac Jacob Reines** after the **First Zionist Congress**.

Moshav (Plural: Moshavot) • Collective settlements in **Palestine** where some property is held in common and some privately.

Moshiach • **Yiddish** and Hebrew for "The Messiah."

Musaf • An additional service on Shabbat morning that is related to the **Musaf** (additional) sacrifice that was offered in the Temple during the Sabbath.

Musar movement • Begun in the nineteenth century by **Rabbi Israel Salanter** his movement emphasized ethical behavior.

Narodnaya Volya • "The People's Will," an anti-Semitic group that encouraged Russian peasants to think of Jews as oppressive landowners and tax collectors; blamed Jews for the death of Alexander II.

Narodniki • Members of **Narodnaya Volya**; Russian nationalists.

National Conference of Russian Jews • Founded in 1905 in Vilna to secure Jewish political and national rights in the new **Duma**.

New Odessa • A kibbutz-like colony in Oregon sponsored by the **Am Olam** movement; failed in 1887.

Nicholas II • **Tzar** of Russia, 1894–1917; abdicated in favor of the **Communists** in that year; later he and his family were murdered.

Okhrana • The tzarist secret police.

ORT • "Society for Manual Labor," founded in 1880 to offer vocational education to Russian Jews; still exists.

Orthodox • Jews who follow the most traditional practices.

Osvobodzhdenie Truda (1883) • "Liberation of Labor Party," the first Russian social democratic organization.

Pale of Settlement • A large section of Poland, western Russia, and adjacent countries where Jews were forcibly concentrated under desperately bad conditions.

Palestine • Today's Israel; the land Jews believe was promised them by God; a homeland where Jews could go for refuge and safety.

Parashah • One of the fifty-four weekly reading sections of the Torah.

Peretz, Isaac Leib (1852–1915) • Writer of stories, songs, and folktales in **Yiddish** that appealed to the average Jewish person.

Pesach • Passover; the festival in the spring that celebrates freedom and the Exodus from Egyptian slavery.

Petach Tikvah • Palestine's first **moshav**, founded in 1878; today a city near Tel Aviv.

Pidyon shevu'im • The redemption or ransom of captives.

Piku'ach nefesh • Saving a life.

Pinsker, Leon (1821–1891) • Wrote **Auto-Emancipation** to advance the idea that Jews should take responsibility for their own future and create a separate Jewish state, where they would be like all other peoples, and then anti-Semitism would cease.

Po'alei Tzion • Organization founded in 1900 in Ekaterinoslav to encourage formation of cooperative settlements of workers in **Palestine**.

Pobedonostsev, Constantine (1827–1907) • Advisor to **Tzars Alexander III** and **Nicholas II** who championed tzarist power, **Orthodox** religion, Russian nationalism, and anti-Semitism; over-procurator of the Holy Synod.

Prospekts • Wide avenues in **St. Petersburg**.

Protocols of the Elders of Zion • A document written in France by the **Okhrana** and then published in Russia in 1903, it claims to tell how an international conspiracy of Jewish leaders plans to take control of the world; an anti-Semitic forgery.

Rabinowitz, Solomon • See **Shalom Aleichem**.

Rakowski, Puah (1865–1955) • **Zionist** and Jewish educator; founder and leader of **Bnos Tzion** and other women's groups.

Rashi (1040–1105) • Rabbi Solomon ben Isaac, often considered the most important commentator on the Bible; lived in the Rhine valley of Germany.

Rebbe • Leader of a **Chasidic** group or dynasty.

Reines, Rabbi Isaac Jacob (1839–1915) • Founded a talmudic academy that also included modern, secular studies to help young Jews compete better in general society; also founded the **Mizrachi** Party.

Rokeach, Joshua (d. 1894) • **Orthodox** rabbi who used his newspaper and organization, Machzikei Da'at, "Upholders of Tradition," to perpetuate traditional Jewish ways.

Russian Social Democratic Labor Party • See **Social Democratic Workers' Party**.

Sadeger *Rebbe* (also pronounced Sadagora) • Leader of a **Chasidic** group that combined religious mysticism and a lavish, regal style of life; wellknown as a patron of Jewish music.

Salanter, Rabbi Israel (1810–1883) • Vilna rabbi who tried to combine ideas of *Mitnagdim* and **Chasidim** into a teaching of ethical and pious behavior.

Schmaltz • Chicken fat that has been melted down and prepared for use in cooking instead of oil.

Schneerson, Rabbi Menachem Mendel (1789–1866) • *Rebbe* of the Lubavitch (**Chabad**) movement.

Second Holy Temple • Built after the Jews returned in 538 B.C.E. from exile in Babylonia, it was destroyed by the Romans in 70 C.E.

Segal, Marc • See **Chagall, Marc**.

Shabbos • Yiddish for "Sabbath."

Shalom Aleichem (1859–1916) • Pen name of Solomon Rabinowitz; author most famous for the character of Tevye the milkman, whose story is the basis of **Fiddler on the Roof.** Also a greeting meaning "Peace to You," the equivalent of "Hello."

Shadchan • Marriage broker.

Shechinah • The Divine Presence that is everywhere and very close to human beings; often considered a more feminine image of God.

Shtetl (Plural: *Shtetlach*) • Small Jewish settlement or village in Eastern Europe.

Shul • Yiddish for "Synagogue."

Shulchan Aruch • A summary of Jewish law written by Joseph Karo (1488–1575) in Safed (Galilee).

Siddur • Prayer book.

Sliosberg, Henry (1863–1937) • Legal advisor to Russian Jewry and **Kadet** member of **Duma.**

Social Democratic Workers' Party • Political party that believed workers should seize control of the government with the guidance of intellectuals and thereby gain full freedom.

Socialist, Socialism • Person or philosophy that believes individuals should control the economy and use its resources equally and fairly for all people; a major political movement in the twentieth century.

Socialist Revolutionary Party • A political party that was part of **Kerensky's** provisional government after the fall of the **tzar**; sided with the **Mensheviks** and was eventually eliminated when the **Bolsheviks** took complete control of Russia.

Streimel • A round fur hat worn by **Chasidic** Jews.

Tallis/tallit • The traditional fringed Jewish prayer shawl, referred to in Numbers 15:37–41.

Talmud • The *Mishnah* and *Gemara* together are the Talmud;sixty-three tractates of Jewish law and ideas collected about 600 C.E. in Babylonia; ever since the basis for traditional Jewish practice.

Tanach • Torah, *Nevi'im* (Prophets) and *Ketuvim* (writings), the three sections that together compose the Jewish Bible.

Tevunah • A magazine published by **Salanter**.

Tishah Be'Av • The ninth day of the month of Av; a sad day commemorating the destruction of the First Temple (586 B.C.E.) and the Second Temple (70 C.E.).

Trotsky, Leon (Davidovich Bronstein) (1879–1940) • Leader of the Communist revolution, who was expelled from power by **Lenin** and later assassinated in Mexico.

Tzar • Ruler of Russia until 1917.

Tzedakah • Hebrew for "charity" or "righteous giving."

Uganda Plan • Proposal in 1903 by Great Britain to create a Jewish homeland in their East African colony of Uganda as a place of refuge for Jews oppressed by pogroms; rejected by **Zionists**.

Vinaver, Maxim (1862–1926) • Founder of the **Constitutional Democratic Party (Kadet)** and representative of the Jews in the **Duma**; lawyer, philanthropist, and advocate for Jewish rights.

Von Plehve, Count Viacheslav (1846–1904) • Tzarist minister of the interior who ruthlessly sought to crush all opposition to the tzarist regime.

Wandering Jew • A figure in Christian legend; a Jew who is condemned constantly to roam the world because he rejected Jesus as the messiah.

Weizmann, Chaim (1874–1952) • Chemist, **Zionist**, first president of the State of Israel.

Western Wall • The only section of the retaining wall of the Second Temple that remains standing in Jerusalem; a place of prayer and hope for Jews.

Winter Palace • The **tzar's** palace in St. Petersburg.

Wise, Rabbi Stephen Samuel (1874–1949) • Reform rabbi who moved from Portland, Oregon to New York City, where he founded the Jewish Institute of Religion and became one of American Jewry's most prominent spokesmen on **Zionist**, Holocaust, and social issues.

Witte, Count Sergei Yulyevich (1849–1915) • Russian advisor to **Tzar Nicholas II**, who urged the **tzar** to adopt more demoractic policies; his counsel was rejected, and he was removed from power.

Yeshivah (Plural: **yeshivot**) • Traditional academy for the study of Talmud and other Jewish subjects.

Yiddish • The daily language spoken by Jews in Eastern Europe; composed of Hebrew, German, and Slavic languages.

Yochanan Ha-Sandlar • A rabbinical disciple of Rabbi Akiba, who lived in Alexandria (Egypt), 100–150 C.E. By profession, he was a shoemaker.

Zalman, Rabbi Schneur (1745–1813) • Founder of **Chabad Chasidism**.

Zhid • Negative word referring to Jews in Polish and Russian.

Zhitlowsky, Chaim (1865–1943) • Early leader of the **Socialist Revolutionary Party**, who held that Jews should become productive workers.

Zion • Israel or the Promised Land, centering on Jerusalem.

Zionist • A person who wishes to establish and support a Jewish home-land in **Zion**.

Zohar • *The Book of Splendor*, the major work of Jewish mysticism written by Moses de Leon in about 1245 in Spain.

Zola, Emile (1840–1902) • French journalist who led efforts to clear **Alfred Dreyfus**.